CHILDCARE ACT

Updated as of March 26, 2018

THE LAW LIBRARY

TABLE OF CONTENTS

Introductory Text	4
Part 1. General functions of local authority: England	4
Interpretation of Part 1	20
Part 2. General Functions of Local Authority: Wales	20
Interpretation of Part 2	24
Part 3. Regulation of Provision of Childcare in England	24
Termination of voluntary registration in Part B of the general childcare register on expiry of prescribed period	82
Power to amend Part 3: applications in respect of multiple premises	83
Interpretation of Part 3	83
Part 3A Inspection of children's centres	84
Part 4. Miscellaneous and General	87
Schedules	93
Schedule 1. Amendments relating to the curriculum	93
Schedule 2. Minor and consequential amendments	95
Schedule 3. Repeals	104
Open Government Licence v3.0	106

Introductory Text

Childcare Act 2006

2006 CHAPTER 21

An Act to make provision about the powers and duties of local authorities and other bodies in England in relation to the improvement of the well-being of young children; to make provision about the powers and duties of local authorities in England and Wales in relation to the provision of childcare and the provision of information to parents and other persons; to make provision about the regulation and inspection of childcare provision in England; to amend Part 10. A of the Children Act 1989 in relation to Wales; and for connected purposes.
[11th July 2006]
Be it enacted by the Queen's most Excellent Majesty, by and with the advice and consent of the Lords Spiritual and Temporal, and Commons, in this present Parliament assembled, and by the authority of the same, as follows:—
Modifications etc. (not altering text)
C1. Act power to amend repealed or modify conferred (conditional) (13.3.2014) by Children and Families Act 2014 (c. 6), s. 137. (2)(5)139. (1)

Part 1. General functions of local authority: England

Part 1. General functions of local authority: England

1. General duties of local authority in relation to well-being of young children

(1) An English local authority must—
    (a) improve the well-being of young children in their area, and
    (b) reduce inequalities between young children in their area in relation to the matters mentioned in subsection (2).
(2) In this Act "well-being", in relation to children, means their well-being so far as relating to—
    (a) physical and mental health and emotional well-being;
    (b) protection from harm and neglect;
    (c) education, training and recreation;
    (d) the contribution made by them to society;
    (e) social and economic well-being.
(3) The Secretary of State may, in accordance with regulations, set targets for—
    (a) the improvement of the well-being of young children in the area of an English local

authority;
   (b) the reduction of inequalities between young children in the area of an English local authority in relation to the matters mentioned in subsection (2).
(4) In exercising their functions, an English local authority must act in the manner that is best calculated to secure that any targets set under subsection (3) (so far as relating to the area of the local authority) are met.
(5) In performing their duties under this section, an English local authority must have regard to any guidance given from time to time by the Secretary of State.
Commencement Information
I1. S. 1 in force at 20.12.2006 for specified purposes by S.I. 2006/3360, art. 2. (a)
I2. S. 1 in force at 1.4.2008 in so far as not already in force by S.I. 2008/785, art. 2. (a)

2. Meaning of "early childhood services" for purposes of section 3.

(1) In section 3 "early childhood services", in relation to an English local authority, means—
   (a) early years provision;
   (b) the social services functions of the local authority, so far as relating to young children, parents or prospective parents;
   (c) health services relating to young children, parents or prospective parents;
   (d) the provision, under arrangements made under section 2 of the Employment and Training Act 1973 (c. 50), of assistance to parents or prospective parents;
   (e) the service provided by the local authority under section 12 (duty to provide information and assistance) so far as relating to parents or prospective parents.
(2) In this section—
"parent" means a parent of a young child, and includes any individual who—
   - has parental responsibility for a young child, or
   - has care of a young child;
"prospective parent" means a pregnant woman or any other person who is likely to become, or is planning to become, a parent;
"social services functions", in relation to a local authority, has the same meaning as in the Local Authority Social Services Act 1970 (c. 42).
Commencement Information
I3. S. 2 in force at 1.4.2008 by S.I. 2008/785, art. 2. (b)

3. Specific duties of local authority in relation to early childhood services

(1) For the purpose of their general duty under section 1. (1), an English local authority have the further duties imposed by subsections (2) and (3).
(2) The authority must make arrangements to secure that early childhood services in their area are provided in an integrated manner which is calculated to—
   (a) facilitate access to those services, and
   (b) maximise the benefit of those services to parents, prospective parents and young children.
(3) The authority must take steps—
   (a) to identify parents or prospective parents in the authority's area who would otherwise be unlikely to take advantage of early childhood services that may be of benefit to them and their young children, and
   (b) to encourage those parents or prospective parents to take advantage of those services.
(4) An English local authority must take all reasonable steps to encourage and facilitate the involvement in the making and implementation of arrangements under this section of—
   (a) parents and prospective parents in their area,

(b) early years providers in their area, including those in the private and voluntary sectors, and

(c) other persons engaged in activities which may improve the well-being of young children in their area.

[F1. (4. A)In deciding what arrangements to make under this section, an English local authority must in particular have regard to—

(a) the quantity and quality of early childhood services that are provided, or that the authority expect to be provided, in their area, and

(b) where in that area those services are provided or are expected to be provided.]

(5) In discharging their duties under this section, an English local authority must have regard to such information about the views of young children as is available to the local authority and appears to them to be relevant to the discharge of those duties.

(6) In discharging their duties under this section, an English local authority must have regard to any guidance given from time to time by the Secretary of State.

(7) In this section—

"early years provider" has the same meaning as in Part 3;

"parent" and "prospective parent" have the same meaning as in section 2.

Amendments (Textual)

F1. S. 3. (4. A) inserted (12.1.2010) by Apprenticeships, Skills, Children and Learning Act 2009 (c. 22), ss. 201, 269. (2)

Commencement Information

I4. S. 3 in force at 1.4.2008 by S.I. 2008/785, art. 2. (b)

4. Duty of local authority and relevant partners to work together

(1) For the purposes of this section each of the following is a relevant partner of an English local authority—

[F2. (za)the National Health Service Commissioning Board;", and]

(a) [F3a clinical commissioning group]F4... F5...for an area any part of which falls within the area of the local authority;3

(b) the Secretary of State, in relation to his functions under section 2 of the Employment and Training Act 1973 (c. 50).

(2) An English local authority must make arrangements to work with each of the authority's relevant partners in the performance by the authority of their duties under sections 1 and 3.

(3) Each of the relevant partners of an English local authority must work with the authority and with the other relevant partners in the making of the arrangements.

(4) An English local authority and each of their relevant partners may for the purposes of arrangements under this section—

(a) provide staff, goods, services, accommodation or other resources;

(b) establish and maintain a pooled fund.

(5) For the purposes of subsection (4) a pooled fund is a fund—

(a) which is made up of contributions by the authority and the relevant partner or partners concerned, and

(b) out of which payments may be made towards expenditure incurred in the discharge of functions of the authority and functions of the relevant partner or partners.

(6) An English local authority and each of their relevant partners falling within subsection (1)(a) must, in exercising their functions under this section, have regard to any guidance given from time to time by the Secretary of State.

Amendments (Textual)

F2. S. 4. (1)(za) inserted (1.4.2013) by Health and Social Care Act 2012 (c. 7), s. 306. (4), Sch. 5 para. 137. (a); S.I. 2013/160, art. 2. (2) (with arts. 7-9)

F3. Words in s. 4. (1)(a) inserted (1.4.2013) by Health and Social Care Act 2012 (c. 7), s. 306. (4), Sch. 5 para. 137. (b)(i); S.I. 2013/160, art. 2. (2) (with arts. 7-9)

F4. Words in s. 4. (1)(a) omitted (1.4.2013) by virtue of Health and Social Care Act 2012 (c. 7), s. 306. (4), Sch. 5 para. 137. (b)(ii); S.I. 2013/160, art. 2. (2) (with arts. 7-9)
F5. Words in s. 4. (1)(a) omitted (1.4.2013) by virtue of Health and Social Care Act 2012 (c. 7), s. 306. (4), Sch. 5 para. 137. (b)(iii); S.I. 2013/160, art. 2. (2) (with arts. 7-9)
Commencement Information
I5. S. 4 in force at 1.4.2008 by S.I. 2008/785, art. 2. (b)
Prospective

5. Power to amend sections 2 and 4.

The Secretary of State may by order—
    (a) amend the definition of "early childhood services" in section 2. (1), and
    (b) in connection with any amendment of that definition, make such other amendments of section 2 or 4 as appear to him to be necessary or expedient.

[F6. Children's centres

Amendments (Textual)
F6. Ss. 5. A-5. G and cross-heading inserted (12.1.2010) by Apprenticeships, Skills, Children and Learning Act 2009 (c. 22), ss. 198, 269. (2)

5. AArrangements for provision of children's centres

(1) Arrangements made by an English local authority under section 3. (2) must, so far as is reasonably practicable, include arrangements for sufficient provision of children's centres to meet local need.
(2) "Local need" is the need of parents, prospective parents and young children in the authority's area.
(3) In determining what provision of children's centres is sufficient to meet local need, an authority may have regard to any children's centres—
    (a) that are provided outside the authority's area, or
    (b) that the authority expect to be provided outside their area.
(4) For the purposes of this Part and Part 3. A a "children's centre" is a place, or a group of places—
    (a) which is managed by or on behalf of, or under arrangements made with, an English local authority, with a view to securing that early childhood services in their area are made available in an integrated manner,
    (b) through which each of the early childhood services is made available, and
    (c) at which activities for young children are provided, whether by way of early years provision or otherwise.
(5) For the purposes of this section, a service is made available—
    (a) by providing the service, or
    (b) by providing advice and assistance to parents and prospective parents on gaining access to the service.
(6) Guidance given under section 3. (6) in respect of arrangements made under section 3. (2) by virtue of subsection (1) of this section may, in particular, relate to—
    (a) circumstances in which any early childhood services should be made available through children's centres as mentioned in subsection (5)(a);
    (b) circumstances in which any early childhood services should be made available through children's centres as mentioned in subsection (5)(b).
(7) A children's centre provided by virtue of arrangements made by an English local authority

under section 3. (2) is to be known as a Sure Start Children's Centre.

5. BChildren's centres: staffing, organisation and operation

(1) Regulations may make provision about the staffing, organisation and operation of children's centres.
(2) The regulations may in particular—
   (a) require English local authorities to secure that children's centres have governing bodies;
   (b) impose obligations and confer powers on any such governing bodies.

5. CChildren's centres: advisory boards

(1) This section applies where arrangements made by an English local authority under section 3.
(2) include arrangements for the provision of one or more children's centres.
(2) The authority must make arrangements to secure that each of the children's centres is within the remit of an advisory board.
(3) A children's centre is within the remit of an advisory board if it is specified in relation to the board by the responsible authority.
(4) An advisory board must provide advice and assistance for the purpose of ensuring the effective operation of the children's centres within its remit.
(5) An advisory board must include persons representing the interests of—
   (a) each children's centre within its remit;
   (b) the responsible authority;
   (c) parents or prospective parents in the responsible authority's area.
(6) An advisory board may also include persons representing the interests of any other persons or bodies that the responsible authority think appropriate.
(7) In exercising their functions under this section, an English local authority must have regard to any guidance given from time to time by the Secretary of State.
(8) The guidance may in particular relate to—
   (a) the membership of advisory boards;
   (b) the organisation and operation of advisory boards.
(9) The " responsible authority ", in relation to an advisory board in respect of which arrangements have been made under subsection (2), is the authority that made the arrangements.

5. DChildren's centres: consultation

(1) An English local authority must secure that such consultation as they think appropriate is carried out—
   (a) before making arrangements under section 3. (2) for the provision of a children's centre;
   (b) before any significant change is made in the services provided through a relevant children's centre;
   (c) before anything is done that would result in a relevant children's centre ceasing to be a children's centre.
(2) In discharging their duty under this section, an English local authority must have regard to any guidance given from time to time by the Secretary of State.
(3) For the purposes of this section a change in the manner in which, or the location at which, services are provided is to be treated as a change in the services.
(4) A " relevant children's centre ", in relation to an authority, is a children's centre provided by virtue of arrangements made by the authority under section 3. (2).

5. EDuty to consider providing services through a children's

centre

(1) This section applies where arrangements made by an English local authority under section 3.
(2) include arrangements for the provision of one or more children's centres.
(2) The authority must consider whether each of the early childhood services to be provided by them should be provided through any of those children's centres.
(3) Each relevant partner of the authority must consider whether each of the early childhood services to be provided by it in the authority's area should be provided through any of those children's centres.
(4) In discharging their duties under this section, the authority and each relevant partner must take into account whether providing a service through any of the children's centres in question would—
    (a) facilitate access to it, or
    (b) maximise its benefit to parents, prospective parents and young children.
(5) In discharging their duties under this section, an English local authority and each of their relevant partners must have regard to any guidance given from time to time by the Secretary of State.
(6) For the purposes of this section, early childhood services are provided by a person or body if they are provided on behalf of, or under arrangements made with, that person or body.
(7) For the avoidance of doubt, nothing in this section is to be taken as preventing an English local authority or any of their relevant partners from providing early childhood services otherwise than through a children's centre.

5. FChildren's centres: transitional provision

(1) This section applies if immediately before the commencement date an English local authority has made arrangements for the provision of a children's centre.
(2) To the extent that this would not otherwise be the case, the arrangements are to be treated for the purposes of this Part and Part 3. A as made under section 3. (2).
(3) "The commencement date" is the day on which section 198 of the Apprenticeships, Skills, Children and Learning Act 2009 comes into force.

5. GChildren's centres: interpretation

In sections 5. A to 5. F—
" children's centre " has the meaning given by section 5. A(4);
" early childhood services " has the same meaning as in section 3;
" parent " and " prospective parent " have the same meaning as in section 2;
" relevant partner " has the same meaning as in section 4.]

Provision of childcare

6. Duty to secure sufficient childcare for working parents

(1) An English local authority must secure, so far as is reasonably practicable, that the provision of childcare (whether or not by them) is sufficient to meet the requirements of parents in their area who require childcare in order to enable them—
    (a) to take up, or remain in, work, or
    (b) to undertake education or training which could reasonably be expected to assist them to obtain work.
(2) In determining for the purposes of subsection (1) whether the provision of childcare is

sufficient to meet those requirements, a local authority—
   (a) must have regard to the needs of parents in their area for—
(i) the provision of childcare in respect of which the child care element of working tax credit is payable, and
[F7. (ia)the provision of childcare in respect of which an amount in respect of childcare costs may be included under section 12 of the Welfare Reform Act 2012 in the calculation of an award of universal credit, and]
(ii) the provision of childcare which is suitable for disabled children, and
   (b) may have regard to any childcare which they expect to be available outside their area.
(3) In discharging their duty under subsection (1), a local authority must have regard to any guidance given from time to time by the Secretary of State.
(4) The Secretary of State may by order amend subsection (2) (and subsection (6) so far as relating to that subsection) so as to modify the matters to which a local authority must or may have regard in determining whether the provision of childcare is sufficient.
(5) Except in relation to a disabled child, this section does not apply in relation to childcare for a child on or after the 1st September next following the date on which he attains the age of 14.
(6) In this section—
"child care element", in relation to working tax credit, is to be read in accordance with section 12 of the Tax Credits Act 2002 (c. 21);
"disabled child" means a child who has a disability for the purposes of the [F8. Equality Act 2010];
"parent" includes any individual who—
   - has parental responsibility for a child, or
   - has care of a child.
Amendments (Textual)
F7. S. 6. (2)(a)(ia) inserted (29.4.2013) by The Universal Credit (Consequential, Supplementary, Incidental and Miscellaneous Provisions) Regulations 2013 (S.I. 2013/630), regs. 1. (2), 19. (2)
F8. Words in s. 6. (6) substituted by 2010 c. 15 Sch. 26 Pt. 1 para. 88 (as inserted) (1.10.2010) by The Equality Act 2010 (Consequential Amendments, Saving and Supplementary Provisions) Order 2010 (S.I. 2010/2279), art. 1. (2), Sch. 1 para. 6 (see S.I. 2010/2317, art. 2)
Commencement Information
I6. S. 6 in force at 1.4.2008 by S.I. 2008/785, art. 2. (b)

[F9 7 Duty to secure early years provision free of charge in accordance with regulations

(1) An English local authority must secure that early years provision of such description as may be prescribed is available free of charge, in accordance with any regulations under this subsection, for each young child in their area who—
   (a) is under compulsory school age, and
   (b) is of such description as may be prescribed.
(2) Regulations under subsection (1) may in particular include provision about—
   (a) how much early years provision is to be made available in pursuance of the duty imposed by subsection (1);
   (b) the times at which, and periods over which, early years provision is to be made available in pursuance of that duty.
(3) In discharging the duty under subsection (1) a local authority must have regard to any guidance given from time to time by the Secretary of State.]
Amendments (Textual)
F9. S. 7 substituted (1.9.2012 for specified purposes, 1.9.2013 in so far as not already in force) by Education Act 2011 (c. 21), ss. 1. (2), 82. (3); S.I. 2012/1087, art. 3; S.I. 2012/2213, art. 5
Commencement Information

I7 S. 7 in force at 1.4.2008 for specified purposes by S.I. 2008/785 , art. 2. (a)
I8 S. 7 in force at 1.9.2008 in so far as not already in force by S.I. 2008/2261 , art 2 (with Sch. 1)

[F107. ADischarge of duty under section 7.

(1) Regulations may require an English local authority to discharge its duty to a young child under section 7 by making arrangements which secure that an early years provider chosen by a parent of the child provides the early years provision to which the child is entitled in cases where—
    (a) the early years provider is willing to provide it, and
    (b) the early years provider is also willing to accept—
(i) any terms as to the payments which would be made to him or her in respect of the provision, and
(ii) any requirements which would be imposed in respect of it.
(2) Arrangements made by an authority to satisfy any requirement imposed under subsection (1) may be made with an early years provider or with an early years childminder agency or any other person who is able to arrange for an early years provider to provide early years provision.
(3) The regulations may provide that such a requirement—
    (a) applies only if the early years provider is of a prescribed description;
    (b) applies only if the early years provision provided by the early years provider is of a prescribed description;
    (c) does not apply in prescribed circumstances.
(4) The regulations may provide that arrangements made by an authority for the purpose of complying with such a requirement must include provision allowing the local authority to terminate the arrangements in prescribed circumstances.
(5) In this section—
"early years childminder agency" and "early years provider" have the same meanings as in Part 3;
"parent" has the same meaning as in section 2.]
Amendments (Textual)
F10. S. 7. A inserted (13.5.2014) by Children and Families Act 2014 (c. 6), ss. 87. (2), 139. (6); S.I. 2014/889, art. 5. (d)

8. Powers of local authority in relation to the provision of childcare

(1) An English local authority may—
    (a) assist any person who provides or proposes to provide childcare;
    (b) make arrangements with any other person for the provision of childcare;
    (c) subject to subsection (3), provide childcare.
(2) The assistance which a local authority may give under subsection (1)(a) includes financial assistance; and the arrangements which a local authority may make under subsection (1)(b) include arrangements involving the provision of financial assistance by the authority.
(3) An English local authority may not provide childcare for a particular child or group of children unless the local authority are satisfied—
    (a) that no other person is willing to provide the childcare (whether in pursuance of arrangements made with the authority or otherwise), or
    (b) if another person is willing to do so, that in the circumstances it is appropriate for the local authority to provide the childcare.
(4) Subsection (3) does not affect the provision of childcare by the governing body of a maintained school.
(5) Subsection (3) does not apply in relation to the provision of childcare under section 18. (1) or (5) of the Children Act 1989 (c. 41) (day care for children in need).

(6) In exercising their functions under this section, an English local authority must have regard to any guidance given from time to time by the Secretary of State.
Commencement Information
I9. S. 8 in force at 1.10.2007 by S.I. 2007/2717, art. 2. (a)

9. Arrangements between local authority and childcare providers

(1) This section applies where an English local authority make arrangements with a person (other than the governing body of a maintained school) for the provision by that person of childcare in consideration of financial assistance provided by the authority under the arrangements.
(2) The local authority must exercise their functions with a view to securing that the provider of the childcare meets any requirements imposed on him by the arrangements.
(3) The requirements imposed by the arrangements may, in particular, if any specified conditions are not satisfied, require the repayment of the whole or any part of any financial assistance provided by the local authority under the arrangements.
Commencement Information
I10. S. 9 in force at 1.10.2007 by S.I. 2007/2717, art. 2. (a)

[F119. AArrangements made by local authorities for the purposes of section 7.

Regulations may provide that arrangements made by an English local authority for the purpose of discharging its duty under section 7—
  (a) may impose requirements on the person with whom the arrangements are made only if the requirements are of a prescribed description;
  (b) may not impose requirements of a prescribed description on the person with whom the arrangements are made.]
Amendments (Textual)
F11. S. 9. A inserted (13.5.2014) by Children and Families Act 2014 (c. 6), ss. 87. (3), 139. (6); S.I. 2014/889, art. 5. (d)

10. Charges where local authority provide childcare

(1) An English local authority may enter into an agreement under which payments are made to the authority for the provision by the authority of childcare for a child.
(2) Subsection (1) does not apply—
  (a) to childcare provided in pursuance of the duty imposed by section 7, or
  (b) to childcare provided under section 18. (1) or (5) of the Children Act 1989 (c. 41) (day care for children in need), provision as to charges for such care being made by section 29 of that Act.
Commencement Information
I11. S. 10 in force at 1.10.2007 by S.I. 2007/2717, art. 2. (a)

F1211. Duty to assess childcare provision

. . . .
Amendments (Textual)
F12. S. 11 repealed (13.5.2014) by Children and Families Act 2014 (c. 6), ss. 86, 139. (6); S.I. 2014/889, art. 5. (d)

Information, advice and assistance

12. Duty to provide information, advice and assistance

(1) An English local authority must establish and maintain a service providing information, advice and assistance in accordance with this section.
(2) The service must provide to parents or prospective parents information which is of a prescribed description and relates to any of the following—
   (a) the provision of childcare in the area of the local authority;
   (b) any other services or facilities, or any publications, which may be of benefit to parents or prospective parents in their area;
   (c) any other services or facilities, or any publications, which may be of benefit to children or young persons in their area.
(3) In prescribing information for the purpose of subsection (2), the Secretary of State must have regard to the needs of the parents of disabled children or young persons for information relating to—
   (a) the provision of childcare which is suitable for disabled children, and
   (b) other services or facilities, or publications, which may be of particular benefit to the parents of disabled children or young persons or to disabled children or young persons.
(4) The service may, in addition to providing information which it is required to provide under subsection (2), provide information relating to any of the matters mentioned in paragraphs (a) to (c) of that subsection to such persons as the local authority consider appropriate.
(5) The service must provide advice and assistance to parents or prospective parents who use, or propose to use, childcare provided in the area of the local authority.
(6) The service must be established and maintained in the manner which is best calculated to facilitate access to the service by persons in the local authority's area who may benefit from it, including, in particular, persons who might otherwise have difficulty in taking advantage of the service.
[F13. (6. A)Regulations may require each English local authority to publish information which is of a prescribed description and relates to any of the matters mentioned in paragraphs (a) to (c) of subsection (2).
(6. B)Regulations under subsection (6. A) may require information to be published—
   (a) at prescribed intervals;
   (b) in a prescribed manner.
(6. C)Subsection (3) applies in relation to information prescribed under subsection (6. A) as it applies in relation to information prescribed under subsection (2).]
(7) In exercising their functions under this section, a local authority must have regard to any guidance given from time to time by the Secretary of State.
(8) For the purposes of this section, a child or young person is disabled if he has a disability for the purposes of the [F14. Equality Act 2010].
(9) In this section—
"parent" means a parent of a child or young person and includes any individual who—
   - has parental responsibility for a child, or
   - has care of a child;
"prospective parent" means a pregnant woman or any other person who is likely to become, or is planning to become, a parent;
"young person" means a person who has attained the age of 18 but has not attained the age of 20.
Amendments (Textual)
F13. S. 12. (6. A)-(6. C) inserted (3.11.2016) by Childcare Act 2016 (c. 5), ss. 5, 7. (2); S.I. 2016/1055, reg. 2. (e)
F14. Words in s. 12. (8) substituted by 2010 c. 15 Sch. 26 Pt. 1 para. 89 (as inserted) (1.10.2010) by The Equality Act 2010 (Consequential Amendments, Saving and Supplementary Provisions)

Order 2010 (S.I. 2010/2279), art. 1. (2), Sch. 1 para. 6 (see S.I. 2010/2317, art. 2)
Commencement Information
I12. S. 12 in force at 20.12.2006 for specified purposes by S.I. 2006/3360, art. 2. (a)
I13. S. 12 in force at 1.5.2007 for specified purposes by S.I. 2007/1019, art. 5
I14. S. 12 in force at 1.4.2008 in so far as not already in force by S.I. 2008/785, art. 2. (a)

13. Duty to provide information, advice and training to childcare providers

(1) An English local authority must, in accordance with regulations, secure the provision of information, advice and training to—
   (a) persons providing childcare in their area who are registered under Part 3;
   (b) persons who intend to provide childcare in their area in respect of which they will be required to be registered under Part 3;
   (c) persons who provide childcare at any of the following [F15institutions] in their area (whether or not they are required to be registered under Part 3)—
(i) a maintained school,
(ii) a school [F16approved] under section 342 of the Education Act 1996 (c. 56) (approval of non-maintained special schools),
(iii) [F17an independent educational institution] [F18or an alternative provision Academy that is not an independent school];
   (d) persons who intend to provide childcare at any such [F19institution] (whether or not they would be required to be registered under Part 3);
   (e) persons who are employed to assist any such persons as are mentioned in paragraph (a) or (c) in the provision of childcare or persons who intend to obtain such employment.
(2) An English local authority may, in addition to securing the provision of information, advice and training which they are required to secure under subsection (1), provide other information, advice and training to any persons mentioned in paragraphs (a) to (e) of that subsection.
(3) An English local authority may provide information, advice and training to persons who do not fall within any of paragraphs (a) to (e) of subsection (1) but who—
   (a) provide or intend to provide childcare in their area, or
   (b) are employed to assist in the provision of childcare in their area or who intend to obtain such employment.
(4) An English local authority may impose such charges as they consider reasonable for the provision of information, advice or training provided by them in pursuance of subsection (1), (2) or (3).
(5) In exercising their functions under this section, an English local authority must have regard to any guidance given from time to time by the Secretary of State.
Amendments (Textual)
F15. Word in s. 13. (1)(c) substituted (5.1.2015) by Education and Skills Act 2008 (c. 25), s. 173. (4), Sch. 1 para. 31. (2)(a); S.I. 2014/3364, art. 2. (z)
F16. Word in s. 13. (1)(c)(ii) substituted (5.1.2015) by Education and Skills Act 2008 (c. 25), s. 173. (4), Sch. 1 para. 31. (2)(b); S.I. 2014/3364, art. 2. (z)
F17. Words in s. 13. (1)(c)(iii) substituted (5.1.2015) by Education and Skills Act 2008 (c. 25), s. 173. (4), Sch. 1 para. 31. (2)(c); S.I. 2014/3364, art. 2. (z)
F18. Words in s. 13. (1)(c)(iii) inserted (1.4.2012) by The Alternative Provision Academies (Consequential Amendments to Acts) (England) Order 2012 (S.I. 2012/976), art. 1, Sch. para. 17 (with art. 3)
F19. Word in s. 13. (1)(d) substituted (5.1.2015) by Education and Skills Act 2008 (c. 25), s. 173. (4), Sch. 1 para. 31. (3); S.I. 2014/3364, art. 2. (z)
Commencement Information
I15. S. 13 in force at 20.12.2006 for specified purposes by S.I. 2006/3360, art. 2. (a)

I16. S. 13 in force at 1.10.2007 in so far as not already in force by S.I. 2007/2717, art. 2. (b)

[F2013. ASupply of information: free of charge early years provision

(1) This subsection applies to information held for the purposes of functions relating to tax credits—
(a) by the Commissioners for Her Majesty's Revenue and Customs, or
(b) by a person providing services to them, in connection with the provision of those services.
(2) This subsection applies to information held for the purposes of functions relating to social security—
(a) by the Secretary of State, or
(b) by a person providing services to the Secretary of State, in connection with the provision of those services.
(3) Information to which subsection (1) or (2) applies may be supplied to the Secretary of State, or a person providing services to the Secretary of State, for use for the purpose of determining eligibility for free of charge early years provision [F21or for funding related to free of charge early years provision].
(4) Information to which subsection (2) applies may be supplied to an English local authority for use for that purpose.
(5) Information received by virtue of subsection (3) may be supplied—
(a) to another person to whom it could have been supplied under that subsection, or
(b) to an English local authority,
for use for that purpose.
(6) The references in subsections (4) and (5)(b) to an English local authority include references to a person exercising on behalf of an English local authority functions relating to eligibility for free of charge early years provision [F22or for funding related to free of charge early years provision].
(7) For the purposes of this section and section 13. B, free of charge early years provision is early years provision which is required to be made available in pursuance of the duty imposed by section 7.
(8) This section does not limit the circumstances in which information may be supplied apart from this section.
Amendments (Textual)
F20. S. 13. A - S. 13. B inserted (1.9.2012) by Education Act 2011 (c. 21), ss. 1. (3), 82. (3); S.I. 2012/1087, art. 3
F21. Words in s. 13. A(3) inserted (26.3.2015) by Small Business, Enterprise and Employment Act 2015 (c. 26), ss. 74. (1)(a), 164. (2)(c)
F22. Words in s. 13. A(6) inserted (26.3.2015) by Small Business, Enterprise and Employment Act 2015 (c. 26), ss. 74. (1)(b), 164. (2)(c)

13. BUnauthorised disclosure of information received under section 13. A

(1) A person commits an offence if the person discloses any information—
(a) which the person received by virtue of any of subsections (3) to (5) of section 13. A, and
(b) which relates to a particular person,
unless the information is disclosed in accordance with subsection (2).
(2) Information is disclosed in accordance with this subsection if it is disclosed in any of the following ways—
(a) in the case of information received by virtue of section 13. A(3), in accordance with section 13. A(5);

(b) in the course of a duty that the person disclosing it has in connection with the exercise of functions relating to eligibility for free of charge early years provision [F23or for funding related to free of charge early years provision];

(c) in accordance with an enactment or an order of a court;

(d) with consent given by or on behalf of the person to whom the information relates.

(3) It is a defence for a person charged with an offence under subsection (1) to prove that the person reasonably believed that the disclosure was lawful.

(4) A person guilty of an offence under subsection (1) is liable—

(a) on conviction on indictment, to imprisonment for a term not exceeding two years, or a fine, or both;

(b) on summary conviction, to imprisonment for a term not exceeding 12 months, or a fine not exceeding the statutory maximum, or both.

(5) In relation to an offence committed before the commencement of section 154. (1) of the Criminal Justice Act 2003, the reference in subsection (4)(b) to 12 months is to be read as a reference to 6 months.]

Amendments (Textual)

F20. S. 13. A - S. 13. B inserted (1.9.2012) by Education Act 2011 (c. 21), ss. 1. (3), 82. (3); S.I. 2012/1087, art. 3

F23. Words in s. 13. B(2)(b) inserted (26.3.2015) by Small Business, Enterprise and Employment Act 2015 (c. 26), ss. 74. (2), 164. (2)(c)

Miscellaneous

Prospective

F2414. Inspection

. . . .

Amendments (Textual)

F24. S. 14 repealed (1.4.2007) by Education and Inspections Act 2006 (c. 40), s. 188. (3), Sch. 14 para. 109, Sch. 18 Pt. 5; S.I. 2007/935, art. 5. (gg)(ii)

15. Powers of Secretary of State to secure proper performance etc.

[F25. (1)Section 496 of the 1996 Act (powers of Secretary of State to prevent unreasonable exercise of functions) applies in relation to the powers conferred or duties imposed on an English local authority by or under this Part as it applies in relation to the powers conferred or duties imposed on a local authority in England by or under the 1996 Act.]

(2) Section 497 of the 1996 Act (general default powers) applies in relation to the duties imposed on an English local authority by or for the purposes of this Part as it applies in relation to the duties imposed on a [F26local authority in England] by or for the purposes of the 1996 Act.

[F27. (3)Section 497. A of the 1996 Act (power to secure proper performance of a local authority's education functions) applies in relation to an English local authority's functions under this Part as it applies in relation to the education functions of a local authority in England.

(3. A)In subsection (3) "education functions" has the meaning given by section 579. (1) of the 1996 Act.]

(4) Sections 497. AA and 497. B of the 1996 Act apply accordingly where powers under section 497. A of that Act are exercised in relation to any of the functions of an English local authority under this Part.

F28. (5). . . . .

(6) In subsection (5) of section 497. A of the 1996 Act, the reference to functions to which that

section applies includes (for all purposes) functions of an English local authority under this Part.
[F29. (6. A)If any functions of an English local authority under this Part are exercisable by a combined authority by virtue of section 105 of the Local Democracy, Economic Development and Construction Act 2009—

(a) a reference in any of subsections (3) to (6) to an English local authority includes a reference to the combined authority, and

(b) a reference in those subsections to functions under this Part is, in relation to the combined authority, to be read as a reference to those functions so far as exercisable by the combined authority.]

(7) In this section, "the 1996 Act" means the Education Act 1996 (c. 56).

Amendments (Textual)

F25. S. 15. (1) substituted (5.5.2010) by The Local Education Authorities and Children's Services Authorities (Integration of Functions) Order 2010 (S.I. 2010/1158), art. 1, Sch. 2 para. 58. (2)(a)

F26. Words in s. 15. (2) substituted (5.5.2010) by The Local Education Authorities and Children's Services Authorities (Integration of Functions) Order 2010 (S.I. 2010/1158), art. 1, Sch. 2 para. 58. (2)(b)

F27 S. 15. (3)(3. A) substituted for s. 15. (3) (5.5.2010) by The Local Education Authorities and Children's Services Authorities (Integration of Functions) Order 2010 (S.I. 2010/1158), art. 1, Sch. 2 para. 58. (2)(c)

F28. S. 15. (5) repealed (5.5.2010) by The Local Education Authorities and Children's Services Authorities (Integration of Functions) Order 2010 (S.I. 2010/1158), art. 1, Sch. 2 para. 58. (2)(d), Sch. 3 Pt. 2

F29. S. 15. (6. A) inserted (31.10.2017) by Children and Social Work Act 2017 (c. 16), ss. 33. (2), 70. (2); S.I. 2017/918, reg. 2. (c)

Modifications etc. (not altering text)

C1. S. 15 modified (3.11.2016) by Childcare Act 2016 (c. 5), ss. 2. (7), 7. (2); S.I. 2016/1055, reg. 2. (b)

Commencement Information

I17. S. 15 in force at 1.4.2007 by S.I. 2007/1019, art. 3

16. Amendments of Children Act 2004.

(1) The Children Act 2004 (c. 31) is amended as follows.

(2) In section 18 (director of children's services), in subsection (2)—

(a) omit the "and" at the end of paragraph (d), and

(b) after paragraph (e) insert "; and

(f) the functions conferred on the authority under Part 1 of the Childcare Act 2006."

(3) In section 23 (interpretation), in subsection (3) (which defines "children's services")—

(a) omit the "and" at the end of paragraph (b), and

(b) after paragraph (c) insert "; and

(d) any function conferred on a local authority under Part 1 of the Childcare Act 2006."

Commencement Information

I18. S. 16 in force at 1.4.2007 by S.I. 2007/1019, art. 3

17. Charges for early years provision at maintained school

(1) Section 451 of the Education Act 1996 (prohibition of charges for provision of education) is amended as follows.

(2) After subsection (2) insert—

"(2. A)Regulations may, in relation to England, prescribe circumstances in which subsection (2) does not apply in relation to education which is early years provision (as defined by section 20 of the Childcare Act 2006) other than —

(a) early years provision provided in pursuance of the duty imposed by section 7 of that Act, or
(b) early years provision for a pupil who is of compulsory school age."
(3) In subsection (4) after paragraph (b) insert "or
(c) provided in pursuance of the duty imposed by section 7 of the Childcare Act 2006."
Commencement Information
I19. S. 17 in force at 1.10.2007 by S.I. 2007/2717, art. 2. (a)

Interpretation

18. Meaning of childcare

(1) This section applies for the purposes of this Part and Part 3.
(2) "Childcare" means any form of care for a child and, subject to subsection (3), care includes—
    (a) education for a child, and
    (b) any other supervised activity for a child.
(3) "Childcare" does not include—
    (a) education (or any other supervised activity) provided by a school during school hours for a registered pupil who is not a young child, or
    (b) any form of health care for a child.
(4) "Childcare" does not include care provided for a child by—
    (a) a parent or step-parent of the child;
    (b) a person with parental responsibility for the child;
    (c) a relative of the child;
    (d) a person who is a local authority foster parent in relation to the child;
    (e) a person who is a foster parent with whom the child has been placed by a voluntary organisation;
    (f) a person who fosters the child privately.
(5) "Childcare" does not include care provided for a child if the care—
    (a) is provided in any of the following establishments as part of the establishment's activities—
[F30. (i)a children's home in respect of which a person is registered under Part 2 of the Care Standards Act 2000,]
(ii) a care home,
(iii) a hospital in which the child is a patient,
(iv) a residential family centre, and
    (b) is so provided by the person carrying on the establishment or a person employed to work at the establishment.
(6) The reference in subsection (5)(b) to a person who is employed includes a reference to a person who is employed under a contract for services.
(7) "Childcare" does not include care provided for a child who is detained in—
    (a) a young offender institution, F31...
    (b) a secure training centre [F32, or]
    [F33. (c)a secure college.]
(8) In this section—
    (a) F34... "local authority foster parent", "to foster a child privately" and "voluntary organisation" have the same meaning as in the Children Act 1989 (c. 41);
    (b) "care home", [F35"children's home"] F36... and "residential family centre" have the same meaning as in the Care Standards Act 2000 (c. 14);
    [F37. (ba)"hospital" has the meaning given by section 275 of the National Health Service Act 2006.]
    (c) "relative", in relation to a child, means a grandparent, aunt, uncle, brother or sister, whether of the full blood or half blood or by marriage or civil partnership.

Amendments (Textual)
F30. S. 18. (5)(a)(i) substituted (1.4.2011 for E., 1.12.2017 for W.) by Children and Young Persons Act 2008 (c. 23), s. 44. (4), Sch. 1 para. 19. (2); S.I. 2010/2981, art. 4. (a); S.I. 2017/948, art. 2. (a)
F31. Word in s. 18. (7)(a) omitted (20.3.2015) by virtue of Criminal Justice and Courts Act 2015 (c. 2), s. 95. (1), Sch. 9 para. 21. (a); S.I. 2015/778, art. 2. (1)(c)
F32. Word in s. 18. (7)(b) inserted (20.3.2015) by Criminal Justice and Courts Act 2015 (c. 2), s. 95. (1), Sch. 9 para. 21. (b); S.I. 2015/778, art. 2. (1)(c)
F33. S. 18. (7)(c) inserted (20.3.2015) by Criminal Justice and Courts Act 2015 (c. 2), s. 95. (1), Sch. 9 para. 21. (c); S.I. 2015/778, art. 2. (1)(c)
F34. Words in s. 18. (8)(a) repealed (1.4.2011 for E., 1.12.2017 for W.) by Children and Young Persons Act 2008 (c. 23), s. 44. (4), Sch. 1 para. 19. (3)(a), Sch. 4; S.I. 2010/2981, art. 4. (a)(l); S.I. 2017/948, art. 2. (a)(c)(iv)
F35. Words in s. 18. (8)(b) inserted (1.4.2011 for E., 1.12.2017 for W.) by Children and Young Persons Act 2008 (c. 23), s. 44. (4), Sch. 1 para. 19. (3)(b); S.I. 2010/2981, art. 4. (a); S.I. 2017/948, art. 2. (a)
F36. Word in s. 18. (8)(b) omitted (1.10.2010) by virtue of Health and Social Care Act 2008 (Consequential Amendments No.2) Order 2010 (S.I. 2010/813), arts. 1. (1), 18
F37. S. 18. (8)(ba) inserted (1.10.2010) by Health and Social Care Act 2008 (Consequential Amendments No.2) Order 2010 (S.I. 2010/813), arts. 1. (1), 18
Commencement Information
I20. S. 18 in force at 20.12.2006 by S.I. 2006/3360, art. 2. (b)

19. Meaning of "young child"

For the purposes of this Part and Part 3, a child is a "young child" during the period—
 (a) beginning with his birth, and
 (b) ending immediately before the 1st September next following the date on which he attains the age of five.
Commencement Information
I21. S. 19 in force at 20.12.2006 by S.I. 2006/3360, art. 2. (b)

20. Meaning of "early years provision"

In this Part "early years provision" means the provision of childcare for a young child.
Commencement Information
I22. S. 20 in force at 20.12.2006 by S.I. 2006/3360, art. 2. (b)

21. Interpretation of Part 1.

In this Part—
"childcare" has the meaning given by section 18;
"early years provision" has the meaning given by section 20;
F38...
F38...
"young child" has the meaning given by section 19.
Amendments (Textual)
F38. Words in s. 21 repealed (31.3.2010) by The Apprenticeships, Skills, Children and Learning Act 2009 (Consequential Amendments) (England and Wales) Order 2010 (S.I. 2010/1080), art. 1. (3)(b)(c), Sch. 1 para. 107, Sch. 2 Pt. 3 (with art. 2. (3))
Commencement Information

I23. S. 21 in force at 20.12.2006 by S.I. 2006/3360, art. 2. (b)

Interpretation of Part 1

21. Interpretation of Part 1.

In this Part—
"childcare" has the meaning given by section 18;
"early years provision" has the meaning given by section 20;
F1...
F1...
"young child" has the meaning given by section 19.
Amendments (Textual)
F1. Words in s. 21 repealed (31.3.2010) by The Apprenticeships, Skills, Children and Learning Act 2009 (Consequential Amendments) (England and Wales) Order 2010 (S.I. 2010/1080), art. 1. (3)(b)(c), Sch. 1 para. 107, Sch. 2 Pt. 3 (with art. 2. (3))
Commencement Information
I1. S. 21 in force at 20.12.2006 by S.I. 2006/3360, art. 2. (b)

Part 2. General Functions of Local Authority: Wales

Part 2. General Functions of Local Authority: Wales

22. Duty to secure sufficient childcare for working parents

(1) A Welsh local authority must secure, so far as is reasonably practicable, that the provision of childcare (whether or not by them) is sufficient to meet the requirements of parents in their area who require childcare in order to enable them—
　(a) to take up, or remain in, work, or
　(b) to undertake education or training which could reasonably be expected to assist them to obtain work.
(2) In determining for the purposes of subsection (1) whether the provision of childcare is sufficient to meet those requirements, a local authority—
　(a) must have regard to the needs of parents in their area for—
(i) the provision of childcare in respect of which the child care element of working tax credit is payable,
[F1. (ia)the provision of childcare in respect of which an amount in respect of childcare costs may be included under section 12 of the Welfare Reform Act 2012 in the calculation of universal credit,]
(ii) the provision of childcare which is suitable for disabled children, and
(iii) the provision of childcare involving the use of the Welsh language, and
　(b) may have regard to any childcare which they expect to be available outside their area.
(3) In discharging their duty under subsection (1), a local authority must have regard to any guidance given from time to time by the Assembly.
(4) The Assembly may by order amend subsection (2) (and subsection (6) so far as relating to that

subsection) so as to modify the matters to which a local authority must or may have regard in determining whether the provision of childcare is sufficient.
(5) Except in relation to a disabled child, this section does not apply in relation to childcare for a child on or after the 1st September next following the date on which he attains the age of 14.
(6) In this section—
"child care element", in relation to working tax credit, is to be read in accordance with section 12 of the Tax Credits Act 2002 (c. 21);
"disabled child" means a child who has a disability for the purposes of the [F2. Equality Act 2010];
"parent" includes any individual who—
- has parental responsibility for a child, or
- has care of a child.

Amendments (Textual)
F1. S. 22. (2)(a)(ia) inserted (W.) (17.7.2013) by The Universal Credit (Consequential Provisions) (Childcare, Housing and Transport) (Wales) Regulations 2013 (No. 1788), regs. 1. (1), 4
F2. Words in s. 22. (6) substituted by 2010 c. 15 Sch. 26 Pt. 1 para. 90 (as inserted) (1.10.2010) by The Equality Act 2010 (Consequential Amendments, Saving and Supplementary Provisions) Order 2010 (S.I. 2010/2279), art. 1. (2), Sch. 1 para. 6 (see S.I. 2010/2317, art. 2)
Commencement Information
I1. S. 22 in force at 31.1.2008 by S.I. 2008/17, art. 2. (a)

23. Powers of local authority in relation to the provision of childcare

(1) A Welsh local authority may—
  (a) assist any person who provides or proposes to provide childcare;
  (b) make arrangements with any other person for the provision of childcare;
  (c) provide childcare.
(2) The assistance which a local authority may give under subsection (1)(a) includes financial assistance; and the arrangements which a local authority may make under subsection (1)(b) include arrangements involving the provision of financial assistance by the authority.
(3) In exercising their functions under this section, a Welsh local authority must have regard to any guidance given from time to time by the Assembly.
Commencement Information
I2. S. 23 in force at 31.1.2008 by S.I. 2008/17, art. 2. (a)

24. Arrangements between local authority and childcare providers

(1) This section applies where a Welsh local authority make arrangements with a person (other than the governing body of a maintained school) for the provision by that person of childcare in consideration of financial assistance provided by the authority under the arrangements.
(2) The local authority must exercise their functions with a view to securing that the provider of the childcare meets any requirements imposed on him by the arrangements.
(3) The requirements imposed by the arrangements may, in particular, if any specified conditions are not satisfied, require the repayment of the whole or any part of any financial assistance provided by the local authority under the arrangements.
Commencement Information
I3. S. 24 in force at 31.1.2008 by S.I. 2008/17, art. 2. (a)

25. Charges where local authority provide childcare

(1) A Welsh local authority may enter into an agreement under which payments are made to the authority for the provision by the authority of childcare for a child.
[F3. (2)Subsection (1) does not apply to childcare provided under sections 37 to 39 of the Social Services and Well-being (Wales) Act 2014 (meeting care and support needs of children), provision as to charges for such care being made by Part 5 of that Act.]
Amendments (Textual)
F3. S. 25. (2) substituted (6.4.2016) by The Social Services and Well-being (Wales) Act 2014 (Consequential Amendments) Regulations 2016 (S.I. 2016/413), regs. 2. (1), 232
Commencement Information
I4. S. 25 in force at 31.1.2008 by S.I. 2008/17, art. 2. (a)

26. Power to require local authority to assess childcare provision

(1) The Assembly may by regulations require a Welsh local authority to—
 (a) prepare assessments at prescribed intervals of the sufficiency of the provision of childcare (whether or not by them) in their area;
 (b) review any such assessment prepared by them.
(2) Regulations under subsection (1) may make provision for the manner in which an assessment or review is to be prepared and, in particular, may require the local authority to—
 (a) consult such persons, or persons of such a description, as may be prescribed, and
 (b) have regard to any guidance given from time to time by the Assembly.
(3) Subsection (5) of section 22 applies for the purposes of this section as it applies for the purposes of that section.
Commencement Information
I5. S. 26 in force at 31.1.2008 by S.I. 2008/17, art. 2. (a)

Information, advice and assistance

27. Duty to provide information, advice and assistance

(1) A Welsh local authority must establish and maintain a service providing information, advice and assistance in accordance with this section.
(2) The service must provide to parents or prospective parents information which is of a prescribed description and relates to any of the following—
 (a) the provision of childcare in the area of the local authority;
 (b) any other services or facilities, or any publications, which may be of benefit to parents or prospective parents in their area;
 (c) any other services or facilities, or any publications, which may be of benefit to children or young persons in their area.
(3) In prescribing information for the purpose of subsection (2), the Assembly must have regard to the needs of the parents of disabled children or young persons for information relating to—
 (a) the provision of childcare which is suitable for disabled children, and
 (b) other services or facilities, or publications, which may be of particular benefit to the parents of disabled children or young persons or to disabled children or young persons.
(4) The service may, in addition to providing information which it is required to provide under subsection (2), provide information relating to any of the matters mentioned in paragraphs (a) to (c) of that subsection to such persons as the local authority consider appropriate.
(5) The service must provide advice and assistance to parents or prospective parents who use, or propose to use, childcare provided in the area of the local authority.

(6) The service must be established and maintained in the manner which is best calculated to facilitate access to the service by persons in the local authority's area who may benefit from it, including, in particular, persons who might otherwise have difficulty in taking advantage of the service.
(7) In exercising their functions under this section, a local authority must have regard to any guidance given from time to time by the Assembly.
(8) For the purposes of this section, a child or young person is disabled if he has a disability for the purposes of the [F4. Equality Act 2010].
(9) In this section—
"parent" means a parent of a child or young person and includes any individual who—
- has parental responsibility for a child, or
- has care of a child;

"prospective parent" means a pregnant woman or any other person who is likely to become, or is planning to become, a parent;
"young person" means a person who has attained the age of 18 but has not attained the age of 20.
Amendments (Textual)
F4. Words in s. 27. (8) substituted by 2010 c. 15 Sch. 26 Pt. 1 para. 91 (as inserted) (1.10.2010) by The Equality Act 2010 (Consequential Amendments, Saving and Supplementary Provisions) Order 2010 (S.I. 2010/2279), art. 1. (2), Sch. 1 para. 6 (see S.I. 2010/2317, art. 2)
Commencement Information
I6 S. 27 in force at 31.1.2008 by S.I. 2008/17 , art. 2. (a)

Miscellaneous

28. Inspection

For the purposes of section 38 of the Education Act 1997 (c. 44) (inspection of local education authorities), the functions conferred on a Welsh local authority by or under this Part are to be regarded as [F5education functions (as defined in section 579. (1) of the Education Act 1996)].
Amendments (Textual)
F5. Words in s. 28 substituted (5.5.2010) by The Local Education Authorities and Children's Services Authorities (Integration of Functions) Order 2010 (S.I. 2010/1158), art. 1, Sch. 2 para. 58. (3)
Commencement Information
I7. S. 28 in force at 31.1.2008 by S.I. 2008/17, art. 2. (a)

[F6 29 Powers of intervention of Welsh Ministers etc.

(1) Chapter 2 of Part 2 the School Standards and Organisation (Wales) Act 2013 (intervention in local authorities) applies in relation to a Welsh local authority and the powers conferred or the duties imposed on it by, under or for the purposes of this Part as it applies in relation to the education functions (as defined by section 579. (1) of the Education Act 1996) of such an authority.
(2) In the application of Chapter 2 of Part 2 of the School Standards and Organisation (Wales) Act 2013 by virtue of this section, section 27 of that Act (power to direct exercise of other education functions) has effect as if the reference to education functions included (for all purposes) functions of a Welsh local authority under this Part.]
Amendments (Textual)
F6. S. 29 substituted (20.2.2014) by School Standards and Organisation (Wales) Act 2013 (anaw 1), s. 100. (4), Sch. 5 para. 10; S.I. 2014/178, art. 2. (f) (with art. 3)

Commencement Information

I8. S. 29 in force at 31.1.2008 by S.I. 2008/17, art. 2. (a)

Interpretation

30. Interpretation of Part 2.

In this Part—
"childcare" means—
- child minding or day care within the meaning of [F7. Part 10. A of the Children Act 1989 (c. 41)][F7 Part 2 of the Children and Families (Wales) Measure 2010] in respect of which the provider is required to be registered under that Part;
- care provided by a person of a description approved in accordance with a scheme made by the Assembly under section 12. (5) of the Tax Credits Act 2002 (c. 21);
"prescribed" means prescribed by regulations made by the Assembly.
Amendments (Textual)
F7. Words in s. 30 substituted (W.) (1.4.2011) by Children and Families (Wales) Measure 2010 (nawm 1), s. 75. (3), Sch. 1 para. 22; S.I. 2010/2582, art. 2, Sch. 1 (with Schs. 2 3)
Commencement Information
I9 S. 30 in force at 31.1.2008 by S.I. 2008/17 , art. 2. (b)

Interpretation of Part 2

30. Interpretation of Part 2.

In this Part—
"childcare" means—
- child minding or day care within the meaning of [F1. Part 10. A of the Children Act 1989 (c. 41)][F1 Part 2 of the Children and Families (Wales) Measure 2010] in respect of which the provider is required to be registered under that Part;
- care provided by a person of a description approved in accordance with a scheme made by the Assembly under section 12. (5) of the Tax Credits Act 2002 (c. 21);
"prescribed" means prescribed by regulations made by the Assembly.
Amendments (Textual)
F1. Words in s. 30 substituted (W.) (1.4.2011) by Children and Families (Wales) Measure 2010 (nawm 1), s. 75. (3), Sch. 1 para. 22; S.I. 2010/2582, art. 2, Sch. 1 (with Schs. 2 3)
Commencement Information
I1 S. 30 in force at 31.1.2008 by S.I. 2008/17 , art. 2. (b)

Part 3. Regulation of Provision of Childcare in England

Part 3. Regulation of Provision of Childcare in England

Chapter 1. General functions of Chief Inspector

Prospective

F1 31. General functions of the Chief Inspector

. . . .

Amendments (Textual)

F1. S. 31 repealed (1.4.2007) by Education and Inspections Act 2006 (c. 40), s. 188. (3), Sch. 14 para. 110, Sch. 18 Pt. 5; S.I. 2007/935, art. 5. (gg)(ii)

32. Maintenance of the two childcare registers

(1) The Chief Inspector must maintain two registers.
(2) The first register ("the early years register") is to be a register of [F2—
    (a)]all persons F3... registered as early years childminders or other early years providers [F4by the Chief Inspector for the purposes of Chapter 2] (which provides for the compulsory registration of persons providing early years provision) [F5, and
    (b) all persons registered as early years childminder agencies under Chapter 2. A (which provides for the compulsory registration of persons with whom early years childminders and certain other early years providers may register for the purposes of Chapter 2).]
(3) The second register ("the general childcare register") is to be divided into two Parts.
(4) The first Part ("Part A") is to be a register of [F6—
    (a) all persons F7... registered as later years childminders or other later years providers [F8by the Chief Inspector for the purposes of Chapter 3] (which provides for the compulsory registration of persons providing later years provision for children under the age of eight)] [F9, and
    (b) all persons registered as later years childminder agencies under Chapter 3. A (which provides for the compulsory registration of persons with whom later years childminders and certain other later years providers may register for the purposes of Chapter 3).]
(5) The second Part ("Part B") is to be a register of all persons who are registered as childminders or other childcare providers [F10by the Chief Inspector for the purposes of Chapter 4] (which provides for the voluntary registration of persons providing early years provision or later years provision in respect of which they are not required to be registered under Chapter 2 or 3).

Amendments (Textual)

F2. Words in s. 32. (2) inserted (1.4.2014 for specified purposes, 1.9.2014 in so far as not already in force) by Children and Families Act 2014 (c. 6), s. 139. (6), Sch. 4 para. 2. (2)(a); S.I. 2014/889, arts. 3. (m), 7. (e)

F3. Words in s. 32. (2) omitted (1.4.2014 for specified purposes, 1.9.2014 in so far as not already in force) by virtue of Children and Families Act 2014 (c. 6), s. 139. (6), Sch. 4 para. 2. (2)(b); S.I. 2014/889, arts. 3. (m), 7. (e)

F4. Words in s. 32. (2) substituted (1.4.2014 for specified purposes, 1.9.2014 in so far as not already in force) by Children and Families Act 2014 (c. 6), s. 139. (6), Sch. 4 para. 2. (2)(c); S.I. 2014/889, arts. 3. (m), 7. (e)

F5. S. 32. (2)(b) and word inserted (1.4.2014 for specified purposes, 1.9.2014 in so far as not already in force) by Children and Families Act 2014 (c. 6), s. 139. (6), Sch. 4 para. 2. (3); S.I. 2014/889, arts. 3. (m), 7. (e)

F6. Word in s. 32. (4) inserted (1.4.2014 for specified purposes, 1.9.2014 in so far as not already in force) by Children and Families Act 2014 (c. 6), s. 139. (6), Sch. 4 para. 2. (4)(a); S.I. 2014/889, arts. 3. (m), 7. (e)

F7. Words in s. 32. (4) omitted (1.4.2014 for specified purposes, 1.9.2014 in so far as not already in force) by virtue of Children and Families Act 2014 (c. 6), s. 139. (6), Sch. 4 para. 2. (4)(b); S.I.

2014/889, arts. 3. (m), 7. (e)

F8. Words in s. 32. (4) substituted (1.4.2014 for specified purposes, 1.9.2014 in so far as not already in force) by Children and Families Act 2014 (c. 6), s. 139. (6), Sch. 4 para. 2. (4)(c); S.I. 2014/889, arts. 3. (m), 7. (e)

F9. S. 32. (4)(b) and word inserted (1.4.2014 for specified purposes, 1.9.2014 in so far as not already in force) by Children and Families Act 2014 (c. 6), s. 139. (6), Sch. 4 para. 2. (5); S.I. 2014/889, arts. 3. (m), 7. (e)

F10. Words in s. 32. (5) substituted (1.4.2014 for specified purposes, 1.9.2014 in so far as not already in force) by Children and Families Act 2014 (c. 6), s. 139. (6), Sch. 4 para. 2. (6); S.I. 2014/889, arts. 3. (m), 7. (e)

Commencement Information

I1. S. 32 in force at 6.4.2007 for specified purposes by S.I. 2007/1019, art. 4

I2. S. 32 in force at 1.9.2008 in so far as not already in force by S.I. 2008/2261, art. 2 (with Schs. 1, 2)

Chapter 2. Regulation of early years provision

33. Requirement to register: early years childminders

(1) A person may not provide early years childminding in England unless he is registered [F11as an early years childminder—.
  (a) in the early years register, or
  (b) with an early years childminder agency.]

(2) The Secretary of State may by order provide that, in circumstances specified in the order, subsection (1) does not apply in relation to early years childminding.

(3) The circumstances specified in an order under subsection (2) may relate to one or more of the following matters (among others)—
  (a) the person providing the early years childminding;
  (b) the child or children for whom it is provided;
  (c) the nature of the early years childminding;
  (d) the premises on which it is provided;
  (e) the times during which it is provided;
  (f) the arrangements under which it is provided.

(4) If it appears to the Chief Inspector that a person has provided early years childminding in contravention of subsection (1), he may serve a notice ("an enforcement notice") on the person.

(5) An enforcement notice may be served on a person—
  (a) by delivering it to him, or
  (b) by sending it by post.

(6) An enforcement notice has effect until it is revoked by the Chief Inspector.

(7) A person commits an offence if, at any time when an enforcement notice has effect in relation to him and without reasonable excuse, he provides early years childminding in contravention of subsection (1).

(8) A person guilty of an offence under subsection (7) is liable on summary conviction to a fine not exceeding level 5 on the standard scale.

Amendments (Textual)

F11. Words in s. 33. (1) substituted (1.4.2014 for specified purposes, 1.9.2014 in so far as not already in force) by Children and Families Act 2014 (c. 6), s. 139. (6), Sch. 4 para. 4; S.I. 2014/889, arts. 3. (m), 7. (e)

Modifications etc. (not altering text)

C1. S. 33. (1) excluded (E.W.) (1.9.2008) by Childcare (Exemptions from Registration) Order 2008 (S.I. 2008/979), arts. 1. (1), 2. (1), 3, 6, 8

Commencement Information

I3. S. 33 in force at 1.10.2007 for specified purposes by S.I. 2007/2717, art. 2. (c)

I4. S. 33 in force at 1.9.2008 in so far as not already in force by S.I. 2008/2261, art. 2 (with Schs. 1, 2)

34. Requirement to register: other early years providers

[F12. (1)A person may not provide early years provision on premises in England which are not domestic premises unless the person is registered in the early years register F13....

[F14. (1. ZA)Subsection (1) does not apply in relation to early years provision—

(a) if it is early years childminding in respect of which the person providing it is required to be registered under section 33. (1), or

(b) if it would be early years childminding but for section 96. (5) and in respect of which the person providing it is required to be registered under subsection (1. A).]

(1. A)A person may not provide early years provision F15... in England which would be early years childminding but for section 96. (5) unless the person is registered—

(a) in the early years register F16..., or

(b) with an early years childminder agency F16....]

(2) [F17. Subsections (1) and (1. A) do] not apply in relation to early years provision for a child or children who has (or have) attained the age of [F18two] if—

(a) the provision is made at any of the following [F19institutions] as part of the [F19 institution's] activities—

(i) a maintained school,

(ii) a school [F20approved]under section 342 of the Education Act 1996 (c. 56) (approval of non-maintained special schools), or

(iii) [F21an independent educational institution],

(b) the provision is made by the proprietor of the [F22institution] or a person employed to work at the [F22institution], and

[F23. (c)where the provision is made at a school (including a school that is an independent educational institution)—

(i) the child is a registered pupil at the school, or

(ii) if the provision is made for more than one child, at least one of the children is a registered pupil at the school.]

(3) The Secretary of State may by order provide that, in circumstances specified in the order, [F24subsections (1) and (1. A) do] not apply in relation to early years provision.

(4) The circumstances specified in an order under subsection (3) may relate to one or more of the following matters (among others)—

(a) the person providing the early years provision;

(b) the child or children for whom it is provided;

(c) the nature of the early years provision;

(d) the premises on which it is provided;

(e) the times during which it is provided;

(f) the arrangements under which it is provided.

(5) A person commits an offence if, without reasonable excuse, he provides early years provision in contravention of subsection (1) [F25or (1. A)].

(6) A person guilty of an offence under subsection (5) is liable on summary conviction to a fine not exceeding level 5 on the standard scale.

Amendments (Textual)

F12. S. 34. (1)(1. A) substituted for s. 34. (1) (1.4.2014 for specified purposes, 1.9.2014 in so far as not already in force) by Children and Families Act 2014 (c. 6), s. 139. (6), Sch. 4 para. 5. (2); S.I. 2014/889, arts. 3. (m), 7. (e)

F13. Words in s. 34. (1) omitted (1.1.2016) by virtue of Small Business, Enterprise and Employment Act 2015 (c. 26), s. 164. (1), Sch. 2 para. 2. (a); S.I. 2015/1329, reg. 6. (b)

F14. S. 34. (1. ZA) inserted (1.1.2016) by Small Business, Enterprise and Employment Act 2015 (c. 26), ss. 76. (6)(a), 164. (1); S.I. 2015/1329, reg. 6. (a)

F15. Words in s. 34. (1. A) omitted (1.1.2016) by virtue of Small Business, Enterprise and Employment Act 2015 (c. 26), ss. 76. (6)(b), 164. (1); S.I. 2015/1329, reg. 6. (a)

F16. Words in s. 34. (1. A)(a)(b) omitted (1.1.2016) by virtue of Small Business, Enterprise and Employment Act 2015 (c. 26), s. 164. (1), Sch. 2 para. 2. (b); S.I. 2015/1329, reg. 6. (b)

F17. Words in s. 34. (2) substituted (1.4.2014 for specified purposes, 1.9.2014 in so far as not already in force) by Children and Families Act 2014 (c. 6), s. 139. (6), Sch. 4 para. 5. (3); S.I. 2014/889, arts. 3. (m), 7. (e)

F18. Word in s. 34. (2) substituted (26.5.2015) by Small Business, Enterprise and Employment Act 2015 (c. 26), ss. 75. (1), 164. (3)(e)

F19. Word in s. 34. (2)(a) substituted (5.1.2015) by Education and Skills Act 2008 (c. 25), s. 173. (4), Sch. 1 para. 32. (2)(a); S.I. 2014/3364, art. 2. (z)

F20. Word in s. 34. (2)(a)(ii) substituted (5.1.2015) by Education and Skills Act 2008 (c. 25), s. 173. (4), Sch. 1 para. 32. (2)(b); S.I. 2014/3364, art. 2. (z)

F21. Words in s. 34. (2)(a)(iii) substituted (5.1.2015) by Education and Skills Act 2008 (c. 25), s. 173. (4), Sch. 1 para. 32. (2)(c); S.I. 2014/3364, art. 2. (z)

F22. Word in s. 34. (2)(b) substituted (5.1.2015) by Education and Skills Act 2008 (c. 25), s. 173. (4), Sch. 1 para. 32. (3); S.I. 2014/3364, art. 2. (z)

F23. S. 34. (2)(c) substituted (5.1.2015) by Education and Skills Act 2008 (c. 25), s. 173. (4), Sch. 1 para. 32. (4); S.I. 2014/3364, art. 2. (z)

F24. Words in s. 34. (3) substituted (1.4.2014 for specified purposes, 1.9.2014 in so far as not already in force) by Children and Families Act 2014 (c. 6), s. 139. (6), Sch. 4 para. 5. (4); S.I. 2014/889, arts. 3. (m), 7. (e)

F25. Words in s. 34. (5) inserted (1.4.2014 for specified purposes, 1.9.2014 in so far as not already in force) by Children and Families Act 2014 (c. 6), s. 139. (6), Sch. 4 para. 5. (5); S.I. 2014/889, arts. 3. (m), 7. (e)

Modifications etc. (not altering text)

C2. S. 34. (1) excluded (E.W.) (1.9.2008) by Childcare (Exemptions from Registration) Order 2008 (S.I. 2008/979), arts. 1. (1), 2. (2), arts. 4-9

Commencement Information

I5. S. 34 in force at 1.10.2007 for specified purposes by S.I. 2007/2717, art. 2. (c)

I6. S. 34 in force at 1.9.2008 in so far as not already in force by S.I. 2008/2261, art. 2 (with Schs. 1, 2)

Process of registration

35. Applications for registration: early years childminders

(1) A person who proposes to provide early years childminding in respect of which he is required by section 33. (1) to be registered may make an application [F26— .

(a) to the Chief Inspector for registration as an early years childminder in the early years register, or

(b) to an early years childminder agency for registration with that agency as an early years childminder.]

(2) An application under subsection (1) must—

(a) give any prescribed information about prescribed matters,

(b) give any other information which the Chief Inspector [F27or (as the case may be) the early years childminder agency] reasonably requires the applicant to give, and

(c) [F28 if it is an application to the Chief Inspector,] be accompanied by any prescribed fee.

(3) The Chief Inspector must grant an application under subsection (1) [F29 (a)] if—

(a) the applicant is not disqualified from registration by regulations under section 75, and

(b) it appears to the Chief Inspector that any requirements prescribed for the purposes of this subsection ("the prescribed requirements for registration") are satisfied and are likely to continue to be satisfied.

(4) The Chief Inspector must refuse any application under subsection (1) [F30 (a)] which subsection (3) does not require him to grant.

[F31. (4. A)An early years childminder agency may grant an application under subsection (1)(b) only if—
(a) the applicant is not disqualified from registration by regulations under section 75,
(b) it appears to the agency that the prescribed requirements for registration are satisfied and are likely to continue to be satisfied, and
(c) it appears to the agency that any other reasonable requirements it has imposed are satisfied and are likely to continue to be satisfied.]
(5) The prescribed requirements for registration may include requirements relating to—
(a) the applicant;
[F32. (aa)prohibiting the applicant from being registered in the early years register as an early years childminder if the applicant is registered with a childminder agency;
(ab) prohibiting the applicant from being registered with an early years childminder agency as an early years childminder if the applicant is registered—
(i) with another childminder agency;
(ii) in the early years register or the general childcare register;]
(b) the premises on which the early years childminding is to be provided;
(c) the arrangements for early years childminding on those premises;
(d) any person who may be caring for children on those premises;
(e) any other person who may be on those premises.

Amendments (Textual)
F26. Words in s. 35. (1) substituted (1.4.2014 for specified purposes, 1.9.2014 in so far as not already in force) by Children and Families Act 2014 (c. 6), s. 139. (6), Sch. 4 para. 6. (2); S.I. 2014/889, arts. 3. (m), 7. (e)
F27. Words in s. 35. (2)(b) inserted (1.4.2014 for specified purposes, 1.9.2014 in so far as not already in force) by Children and Families Act 2014 (c. 6), s. 139. (6), Sch. 4 para. 6. (3)(a); S.I. 2014/889, arts. 3. (m), 7. (e)
F28. Words in s. 35. (2)(c) inserted (1.4.2014 for specified purposes, 1.9.2014 in so far as not already in force) by Children and Families Act 2014 (c. 6), s. 139. (6), Sch. 4 para. 6. (3)(b); S.I. 2014/889, arts. 3. (m), 7. (e)
F29. Word in s. 35. (3) inserted (1.4.2014 for specified purposes, 1.9.2014 in so far as not already in force) by Children and Families Act 2014 (c. 6), s. 139. (6), Sch. 4 para. 6. (4); S.I. 2014/889, arts. 3. (m), 7. (e)
F30. Word in s. 35. (4) inserted (1.4.2014 for specified purposes, 1.9.2014 in so far as not already in force) by Children and Families Act 2014 (c. 6), s. 139. (6), Sch. 4 para. 6. (4); S.I. 2014/889, arts. 3. (m), 7. (e)
F31. S. 35. (4. A) inserted (1.4.2014 for specified purposes, 1.9.2014 in so far as not already in force) by Children and Families Act 2014 (c. 6), s. 139. (6), Sch. 4 para. 6. (5); S.I. 2014/889, arts. 3. (m), 7. (e)
F32. S. 35. (5)(aa)(ab) inserted (1.4.2014 for specified purposes, 1.9.2014 in so far as not already in force) by Children and Families Act 2014 (c. 6), s. 139. (6), Sch. 4 para. 6. (6); S.I. 2014/889, arts. 3. (m), 7. (e)

Commencement Information
I7. S. 35 in force at 1.10.2007 for specified purposes by S.I. 2007/2717, art. 2. (c)
I8. S. 35 in force at 1.9.2008 in so far as not already in force by S.I. 2008/2261, art. 2 (with Schs. 1, 2)

36. Applications for registration: other early years providers
(1) A person who proposes to provide F33... early years provision in respect of which he is required by section 34. (1) to be registered may make an application to the Chief Inspector for registration as an early years provider F33....
[F34. (1. A)A person who proposes to provide F35... early years provision in respect of which the person is required by section 34. (1. A) to be registered may make an application—
(a) to the Chief Inspector for registration as an early years provider F36..., or
(b) to an early years childminder agency for registration with that agency as an early years

provider F36....]

(2) An application under subsection (1) [F37or (1. A)] must—

(a) give any prescribed information about prescribed matters,

(b) give any other information which the Chief Inspector [F38or (as the case may be) the early years childminder agency] reasonably requires the applicant to give, and

(c) [F39if it is an application to the Chief Inspector,] be accompanied by any prescribed fee.

(3) The Chief Inspector must grant an application under subsection (1) [F40or (1. A)(a)] if—

(a) the applicant is not disqualified from registration by regulations under section 75, and

(b) it appears to the Chief Inspector that any requirements prescribed for the purposes of this subsection ("the prescribed requirements for registration") are satisfied and are likely to continue to be satisfied.

(4) The Chief Inspector must refuse any application under subsection (1) [F41or (1. A)(a)] which subsection (3) does not require him to grant.

[F42. (4. A)An early years childminder agency may grant an application under subsection (1. A)(b) only if—

(a) the applicant is not disqualified from registration by regulations under section 75,

(b) it appears to the agency that the prescribed requirements for registration are satisfied and are likely to continue to be satisfied, and

(c) it appears to the agency that any other reasonable requirements it has imposed are satisfied and are likely to continue to be satisfied.]

(5) The prescribed requirements for registration may include requirements relating to—

(a) the applicant;

[F43. (aa)prohibiting the applicant from being registered in the early years register as an early years provider other than a childminder if the applicant is registered with a childminder agency;

(ab) prohibiting the applicant from being registered with an early years childminder agency as an early years provider other than a childminder if the applicant is registered—

(i) with another childminder agency;

(ii) in the early years register or the general childcare register;]

(b) the premises on which the early years provision is to be provided;

(c) the arrangements for early years provision on those premises;

(d) any person who may be caring for children on those premises;

(e) any other person who may be on those premises.

Amendments (Textual)

F33. Words in s. 36. (1) omitted (1.1.2016) by virtue of Small Business, Enterprise and Employment Act 2015 (c. 26), s. 164. (1), Sch. 2 para. 3. (a); S.I. 2015/1329, reg. 6. (b)

F34. S. 36. (1. A) inserted (1.4.2014 for specified purposes, 1.9.2014 in so far as not already in force) by Children and Families Act 2014 (c. 6), s. 139. (6), Sch. 4 para. 7. (2); S.I. 2014/889, arts. 3. (m), 7. (e)

F35. Words in s. 36. (1. A) omitted (1.1.2016) by virtue of Small Business, Enterprise and Employment Act 2015 (c. 26), s. 164. (1), Sch. 2 para. 3. (b); S.I. 2015/1329, reg. 6. (b)

F36. Words in s. 36. (1. A)(a)(b) omitted (1.1.2016) by virtue of Small Business, Enterprise and Employment Act 2015 (c. 26), s. 164. (1), Sch. 2 para. 3. (c); S.I. 2015/1329, reg. 6. (b)

F37. Words in s. 36. (2) inserted (1.4.2014 for specified purposes, 1.9.2014 in so far as not already in force) by Children and Families Act 2014 (c. 6), s. 139. (6), Sch. 4 para. 7. (3)(a); S.I. 2014/889, arts. 3. (m), 7. (e)

F38. Words in s. 36. (2)(b) inserted (1.4.2014 for specified purposes, 1.9.2014 in so far as not already in force) by Children and Families Act 2014 (c. 6), s. 139. (6), Sch. 4 para. 7. (3)(b); S.I. 2014/889, arts. 3. (m), 7. (e)

F39. Words in s. 36. (2)(c) inserted (1.4.2014 for specified purposes, 1.9.2014 in so far as not already in force) by Children and Families Act 2014 (c. 6), s. 139. (6), Sch. 4 para. 7. (3)(c); S.I. 2014/889, arts. 3. (m), 7. (e)

F40. Words in s. 36. (3) inserted (1.4.2014 for specified purposes, 1.9.2014 in so far as not already in force) by Children and Families Act 2014 (c. 6), s. 139. (6), Sch. 4 para. 7. (4); S.I. 2014/889, arts. 3. (m), 7. (e)

F41. Words in s. 36. (4) inserted (1.4.2014 for specified purposes, 1.9.2014 in so far as not already in force) by Children and Families Act 2014 (c. 6), s. 139. (6), Sch. 4 para. 7. (4); S.I. 2014/889, arts. 3. (m), 7. (e)

F42. S. 36. (4. A) inserted (1.4.2014 for specified purposes, 1.9.2014 in so far as not already in force) by Children and Families Act 2014 (c. 6), s. 139. (6), Sch. 4 para. 7. (5); S.I. 2014/889, arts. 3. (m), 7. (e)

F43. S. 36. (5)(aa)(ab) inserted (1.4.2014 for specified purposes, 1.9.2014 in so far as not already in force) by Children and Families Act 2014 (c. 6), s. 139. (6), Sch. 4 para. 7. (6); S.I. 2014/889, arts. 3. (m), 7. (e)

Commencement Information

I9. S. 36 in force at 1.10.2007 for specified purposes by S.I. 2007/2717, art. 2. (c)

I10. S. 36 in force at 1.9.2008 in so far as not already in force by S.I. 2008/2261, art. 2 (with Schs. 1, 2)

37. Entry on the register and certificates

(1) If an application under section 35. (1) [F44. (a)] is granted, the Chief Inspector must—
   (a) register the applicant in the early years register as an early years childminder, and
   (b) give the applicant a certificate of registration stating that he is so registered.

(2) If an application under section 36. (1) [F45or (1. A)(a)] is granted, the Chief Inspector must—
   (a) register the applicant in the early years register as an early years provider other than a childminder F46..., and
   (b) give the applicant a certificate of registration stating that he is so registered.

(3) A certificate of registration given to the applicant in pursuance of subsection (1) or (2) must contain prescribed information about prescribed matters.

(4) If there is a change of circumstances which requires the amendment of a certificate of registration, the Chief Inspector must give the registered early years provider an amended certificate.

(5) If the Chief Inspector is satisfied that a certificate of registration has been lost or destroyed, the Chief Inspector must give the registered early years provider a copy, on payment by the provider of any prescribed fee.

Amendments (Textual)

F44. Word in s. 37. (1) inserted (1.4.2014 for specified purposes, 1.9.2014 in so far as not already in force) by Children and Families Act 2014 (c. 6), s. 139. (6), Sch. 4 para. 8. (2); S.I. 2014/889, arts. 3. (m), 7. (e)

F45. Words in s. 37. (2) inserted (1.4.2014 for specified purposes, 1.9.2014 in so far as not already in force) by Children and Families Act 2014 (c. 6), s. 139. (6), Sch. 4 para. 8. (3); S.I. 2014/889, arts. 3. (m), 7. (e)

F46. Words in s. 37. (2)(a) omitted (1.1.2016) by virtue of Small Business, Enterprise and Employment Act 2015 (c. 26), s. 164. (1), Sch. 2 para. 4; S.I. 2015/1329, reg. 6. (b)

Commencement Information

I11. S. 37 in force at 1.10.2007 for specified purposes by S.I. 2007/2717, art. 2. (c)

I12. S. 37 in force at 1.9.2008 in so far as not already in force by S.I. 2008/2261, art. 2 (with Schs. 1, 2)

[F4737. AEarly years childminder agencies: registers and certificates

(1) If an application under section 35. (1)(b) is granted, the early years childminder agency must—
   (a) register the applicant in the register maintained by the agency as an early years childminder, and
   (b) give the applicant a certificate of registration stating that he or she is so registered.

(2) If an application under section 36. (1. A)(b) is granted, the early years childminder agency must—
   (a) register the applicant in the register maintained by the agency as an early years provider other than a childminder F48..., and
   (b) give the applicant a certificate of registration stating that he or she is so registered.

(3) A certificate of registration given to the applicant in pursuance of subsection (1) or (2) must contain prescribed information about prescribed matters.

(4) If there is a change of circumstances which requires the amendment of a certificate of registration, the early years childminder agency must give the registered early years provider an amended certificate.]

Amendments (Textual)

F47. S. 37. A inserted (1.4.2014 for specified purposes, 1.9.2014 in so far as not already in force) by Children and Families Act 2014 (c. 6), s. 139. (6), Sch. 4 para. 9; S.I. 2014/889, arts. 3. (m), 7. (e)

F48. Words in s. 37. A(2)(a) omitted (1.1.2016) by virtue of Small Business, Enterprise and Employment Act 2015 (c. 26), s. 164. (1), Sch. 2 para. 5; S.I. 2015/1329, reg. 6. (b)

38. Conditions on registration

(1) The Chief Inspector may impose such conditions as he thinks fit on the registration of an early years provider [F49in the early years register].

(2) The power conferred by subsection (1) may be exercised at the time when the Chief Inspector registers the person in pursuance of section 37 or at any subsequent time.

(3) The Chief Inspector may at any time vary or remove any condition imposed under subsection (1).

(4) The power conferred by subsection (1) includes power to impose conditions for the purpose of giving effect to an order under subsection (1)(a) of section 39 or regulations under subsection (1)(b) of that section.

F50. (5)An early years provider registered [F51in the early years register] commits an offence if, without reasonable excuse, he fails to comply with any condition imposed under subsection (1).

(6) A person guilty of an offence under subsection (5) is liable on summary conviction to a fine not exceeding level 5 on the standard scale.

Amendments (Textual)

F49. Words in s. 38. (1) substituted (1.4.2014 for specified purposes, 1.9.2014 in so far as not already in force) by Children and Families Act 2014 (c. 6), s. 139. (6), Sch. 4 para. 10; S.I. 2014/889, arts. 3. (m), 7. (e)

F50. Words in s. 38. (5) substituted (1.4.2014 for specified purposes, 1.9.2014 in so far as not already in force) by Children and Families Act 2014 (c. 6), s. 139. (6), Sch. 4 para. 10; S.I. 2014/889, arts. 3. (m), 7. (e)

F51. Words in s. 38. (5) substituted (1.4.2014 for specified purposes) by Children and Families Act 2014 (c. 6), s. 139. (6), Sch. 4 para. 10; S.I. 2014/889, art. 3. (m)

Commencement Information

I13. S. 38 in force at 1.9.2008 by S.I. 2008/2261, art. 2 (with Schs. 1, 2)

Requirements to be met by early years providers

39. The Early Years Foundation Stage

(1) For the purpose of promoting the well-being of young children for whom early years provision is provided by early years providers to whom section 40 applies, the Secretary of State must—

(a) by order specify in accordance with section 41 such requirements as he considers appropriate relating to learning by, and the development of, such children ("learning and development requirements"), and

(b) by regulations specify in accordance with section 43 such requirements as he considers appropriate governing the activities of early years providers to whom section 40 applies ("welfare requirements").

(2) The learning and development requirements and the welfare requirements are together to be known as "the Early Years Foundation Stage".

Commencement Information

I14. S. 39 in force at 20.12.2006 by S.I. 2006/3360, art. 2. (c)

40. Duty to implement Early Years Foundation Stage

(1) This section applies to—

(a) early years providers providing early years provision in respect of which they are registered under this Chapter, and

(b) early years providers providing early years provision in respect of which, but for section 34. (2) (exemption for provision for children aged [F522] or over at certain schools), they would be required to be registered under this Chapter.

(2) An early years provider to whom this section applies—

(a) must secure that the early years provision meets the learning and development requirements, and

(b) must comply with the welfare requirements.

Amendments (Textual)

F52. Figure in s. 40. (1)(b) substituted (26.5.2015) by Small Business, Enterprise and Employment Act 2015 (c. 26), ss. 75. (2), 164. (3)(e)

Commencement Information

I15. S. 40 in force at 1.9.2008 by S.I. 2008/2261, art. 2 (with Schs. 1, 2)

41. The learning and development requirements

(1) The learning and development requirements must cover the areas of learning and development specified in subsection (3).

(2) The learning and development requirements may specify in relation to each of the areas of learning and development—

(a) the knowledge, skills and understanding which young children of different abilities and maturities are expected to have before the 1st September next following the day on which they attain the age of five ("early learning goals");

(b) the matters, skills and processes which are required to be taught to young children of different abilities and maturities ("educational programmes"), and

(c) the arrangements which are required for assessing children [F53for the specified purposes] ("assessment arrangements").

(3) The areas of learning and development are as follows—

(a) personal, social and emotional development,

(b) communication, language and literacy,

(c) problem solving, reasoning and numeracy,

(d) knowledge and understanding of the world,

(e) physical development, and

(f) creative development.

(4) The Secretary of State may by order amend subsection (3).

[F54. (4. A) In subsection (2)(c) " the specified purposes " means—

(a) the purpose of ascertaining what children have achieved in relation to the early learning goals, and

(b) such other purposes as the Secretary of State may by order specify.]

(5) A learning and development order may not require—

(a) the allocation of any particular period or periods of time to the teaching of any educational programme or any matter, skill or process forming part of it, or

(b) the making in the timetables of any early years provider of provision of any particular kind for the periods to be allocated to such teaching.

(6) In this section "a learning and development order" means an order under section 39. (1)(a).

Amendments (Textual)

F53. Words in s. 41. (2)(c) substituted (1.4.2010) by Apprenticeships, Skills, Children and Learning Act 2009 (c. 22), s. 269. (4), Sch. 12 para. 39. (2); S.I. 2010/1151, art. 2, Sch. 1

F54. S. 41. (4. A) inserted (1.4.2010) by Apprenticeships, Skills, Children and Learning Act 2009 (c. 22), s. 269. (4), Sch. 12 para. 39. (3); S.I. 2010/1151, art. 2, Sch. 1

Commencement Information

I16. S. 41 in force at 20.12.2006 by S.I. 2006/3360, art. 2. (c)

42. Further provisions about assessment arrangements

[F55. (A1)Before making a learning and development order specifying assessment arrangements the Secretary of State—

    (a) must consult the Office of Qualifications and Examinations Regulation, and

    (b) may consult such other persons as the Secretary of State considers appropriate.]

(1) A learning and development order specifying assessment arrangements may confer or impose on any of the persons mentioned in subsection (2) such functions as appear to the Secretary of State to be required.

(2) Those persons are—

    (a) an early years provider,

    (b) the governing body or head teacher of a maintained school in England, F56...

    (c) an English local authority.

    F57. (d). . . . .

[F58. (e)any other person with whom the Secretary of State has made arrangements in connection with the development, implementation or monitoring of assessment arrangements.]

(3) A learning and development order may specify such assessment arrangements as may for the time being be made by a person specified in the order.

[F59. (3. A)A learning and development order which includes provision made by virtue of subsection (3) must provide that before making or revising the assessment arrangements the person specified in the order—

    (a) must consult the Office of Qualifications and Examinations Regulation, and

    (b) may consult such other persons as that person considers appropriate.]

F60. (4). . . . .

(5) [F61. The duties that may be imposed on a person mentioned in subsection (2)(a) to (c) by virtue of subsection (1) include, in relation to persons exercising any function in connection with the moderation or monitoring of assessment arrangements, the duty to permit them—]

    (a) to enter premises on which the early years provision is provided,

    (b) to observe implementation of the arrangements, F56...

    (c) to inspect, and take copies of, documents and other articles.

[F62. (6)A learning and development order specifying assessment arrangements may authorise a person specified in the order to make delegated supplementary provisions in relation to such matters as may be specified in the order.

(6. A) In this section " delegated supplementary provisions " means such provisions (other than provisions conferring or imposing functions on persons mentioned in subsection (2)(a) to (c)) as appear to the authorised person to be expedient for giving full effect to, or otherwise supplementing, the provisions made by the order.

[F63. (6. AA)A learning and development order which authorises a person to make delegated supplementary provisions must provide that before making, amending or revoking any such provisions the person so authorised—

    (a) must consult the Office of Qualifications and Examinations Regulation, and

    (b) may consult such other persons as that person considers appropriate.]

(6. B)A learning and development order authorising the making of delegated supplementary provisions may provide that such provisions may be made only with the approval of the Secretary of State.

(6. C)Any delegated supplementary provisions, on being published as specified in the order under which they are made, are to have effect for the purposes of this Chapter as if made by the order.]

(7) In this section "a learning and development order" means an order under section 39. (1)(a).

Amendments (Textual)

F55. S. 42. (A1) inserted (1.4.2010) by Apprenticeships, Skills, Children and Learning Act 2009 (c. 22), ss. 160. (2), 269. (4); S.I. 2010/1151, art. 2, Sch. 1 (with arts. 5-20)

F56. Word in s. 42. (2)(b) repealed (1.4.2010) by Apprenticeships, Skills, Children and Learning Act 2009 (c. 22), s. 269. (4), Sch. 12 para. 40. (2)(a), Sch. 16 Pt. 4; S.I. 2010/1151, art. 2, Sch. 1

F57. S. 42. (2)(d) omitted (1.4.2012) by virtue of Education Act 2011 (c. 21), s. 82. (3), Sch. 8

para. 17; S.I. 2012/924, art. 2

F58. S. 42. (2)(d)(e) inserted (1.4.2010) by Apprenticeships, Skills, Children and Learning Act 2009 (c. 22), s. 269. (4), Sch. 12 para. 40. (2)(b); S.I. 2010/1151, art. 2, Sch. 1

F59. S. 42. (3. A) inserted (1.4.2010 for specified purposes) by Apprenticeships, Skills, Children and Learning Act 2009 (c. 22), ss. 160. (3), 269. (4); S.I. 2010/1151, art. 2, Sch. 1 (with arts. 5-20)

F60. S. 42. (4) repealed (1.4.2010) by Apprenticeships, Skills, Children and Learning Act 2009 (c. 22), s. 269. (4), Sch. 12 para. 40. (3), Sch. 16 Pt. 4; S.I. 2010/1151, art. 2, Sch. 1

F61. Words in s. 42. (5) substituted (1.4.2010) by Apprenticeships, Skills, Children and Learning Act 2009 (c. 22), s. 269. (4), Sch. 12 para. 40. (4); S.I. 2010/1151, art. 2, Sch. 1

F62. S. 42. (6)-(6. C) substituted for s. 42. (6) (1.4.2010) by Apprenticeships, Skills, Children and Learning Act 2009 (c. 22), s. 269. (4), Sch. 12 para. 40. (5); S.I. 2010/1151, art. 2, Sch. 1

F63. S. 42. (6. AA) inserted (1.4.2010 for specified purposes) by Apprenticeships, Skills, Children and Learning Act 2009 (c. 22), ss. 160. (4), 269. (4); S.I. 2010/1151, art. 2, Sch. 1 (with arts. 5-20)

Commencement Information

I17. S. 42 in force at 20.12.2006 by S.I. 2006/3360, art. 2. (c)

43. Welfare requirements

(1) The matters that may be dealt with by welfare regulations include—
   (a) the welfare of the children concerned;
   (b) the arrangements for safeguarding the children concerned;
   (c) suitability of persons to care for, or be in regular contact with, the children concerned;
   (d) qualifications and training;
   (e) the suitability of premises and equipment;
   (f) the manner in which the early years provision is organised;
   (g) procedures for dealing with complaints;
   (h) the keeping of records;
   (i) the provision of information.

(2) Before making welfare regulations, the Secretary of State must consult the Chief Inspector and any other persons he considers appropriate.

(3) Welfare regulations may provide—
   (a) that a person who without reasonable excuse fails to comply with any requirement of the regulations is guilty of an offence, and
   (b) that a person guilty of the offence is liable on summary conviction to a fine not exceeding level 5 on the standard scale.

(4) In this section "welfare regulations" means regulations under section 39. (1)(b).

Commencement Information

I18. S. 43 in force at 20.12.2006 by S.I. 2006/3360, art. 2. (c)

44. Instruments specifying learning and development or welfare requirements

(1) A relevant instrument may, instead of containing the provisions to be made, refer to provisions in a document [F64published by a person, and in the manner, specified] in the instrument and direct that those provisions are to have effect or, as the case may be, are to have effect as specified in the instrument.

(2) The power to make a relevant instrument may be exercised so as to confer powers or impose duties on the Chief Inspector [F65or early years childminder agencies] in the exercise of F66... functions under this Part.

(3) In particular, that power may be exercised so as to require or authorise the Chief Inspector [F67or early years childminder agencies], in exercising those functions, to have regard to factors, standards and other matters prescribed by or referred to in the instrument.

(4) If a relevant instrument requires any person (other than the Chief Inspector) to have regard to or meet factors, standards and other matters prescribed by or referred to in the instrument, the instrument may also provide for any allegation that the person has failed to do so to be taken into account—
   (a) by the Chief Inspector in the exercise of his functions under this Part,
   [F68. (aa)by early years childminder agencies in the exercise of functions under this Part,] or

(b) in any proceedings under this Part.

(5) In this section "a relevant instrument" means an order under subsection (1)(a) of section 39 or regulations under subsection (1)(b) of that section.

Amendments (Textual)

F64. Words in s. 44. (1) substituted (1.4.2010) by Apprenticeships, Skills, Children and Learning Act 2009 (c. 22), s. 269. (4), Sch. 12 para. 41; S.I. 2010/1151, art. 2, Sch. 1

F65. Words in s. 44. (2) inserted (1.4.2014 for specified purposes, 1.9.2014 in so far as not already in force) by Children and Families Act 2014 (c. 6), s. 139. (6), Sch. 4 para. 11. (2)(a); S.I. 2014/889, arts. 3. (m), 7. (e)

F66. Word in s. 44. (2) omitted (1.4.2014 for specified purposes, 1.9.2014 in so far as not already in force) by virtue of Children and Families Act 2014 (c. 6), s. 139. (6), Sch. 4 para. 11. (2)(b); S.I. 2014/889, arts. 3. (m), 7. (e)

F67. Words in s. 44. (3) inserted (1.4.2014 for specified purposes, 1.9.2014 in so far as not already in force) by Children and Families Act 2014 (c. 6), s. 139. (6), Sch. 4 para. 11. (3); S.I. 2014/889, arts. 3. (m), 7. (e)

F68. S. 44. (4)(aa) inserted (1.4.2014 for specified purposes, 1.9.2014 in so far as not already in force) by Children and Families Act 2014 (c. 6), s. 139. (6), Sch. 4 para. 11. (4); S.I. 2014/889, arts. 3. (m), 7. (e)

Commencement Information

I19. S. 44 in force at 20.12.2006 by S.I. 2006/3360, art. 2. (c)

45. Procedure for making certain orders

(1) This section applies where the Secretary of State proposes to make an order under section 39.
(1)(a) specifying early learning goals or educational programmes.

(2) The Secretary of State must give notice of the proposal—

(a) to such bodies representing the interests of early years providers as the Secretary of State considers appropriate, and

(b) to any other persons with whom consultation appears to the Secretary of State to be desirable,

and must give them a reasonable opportunity of submitting evidence and representations as to the issues arising.

(3) When the Secretary of State has considered any evidence and representations submitted to him in pursuance of subsection (2), he must publish in such manner as, in his opinion, is likely to bring them to the notice of persons having a special interest in early years provision—

(a) a draft of the proposed order and any associated document, and

(b) a summary of the views expressed during the consultation.

(4) The Secretary of State must allow a period of not less than one month beginning with the publication of the draft of the proposed order for the submission of any further evidence and representations as to the issues arising.

(5) When the period so allowed has expired, the Secretary of State may make the order, with or without modifications.

Commencement Information

I20. S. 45 in force at 20.12.2006 by S.I. 2006/3360, art. 2. (c)

46. Power to enable exemptions to be conferred

(1) Regulations may enable the Secretary of State, in prescribed circumstances, to direct in respect of a particular early years provider or a particular description of early years providers, that to such extent as may be prescribed the learning and development requirements—

(a) do not apply, or

(b) apply with such modifications as may be specified in the direction.

[F69. (1. A)Regulations under subsection (1) may make provision about the conditions which may be imposed by the Secretary of State on making a direction.

(1. B)If required by the Secretary of State to do so [F70a person designated by the Secretary of State for the purposes of this subsection] must keep under review the effect of a direction given under regulations made under subsection (1).

F71. (1. C)..............................

(1. D)A designation under [F72subsection (1. B)] may make different provision for different purposes.]

(2) Regulations may enable an early years provider, in prescribed circumstances, to determine in respect of a particular young child that to such extent as may be prescribed the learning and development requirements—

(a) do not apply, or

(b) apply with such modifications as may be specified in the determination.

Amendments (Textual)

F69. S. 46. (1. A)-(1. D) inserted (1.4.2010) by Apprenticeships, Skills, Children and Learning Act 2009 (c. 22), s. 269. (4), Sch. 12 para. 42; S.I. 2010/1151, art. 2, Sch. 1

F70. Words in s. 46. (1. B) substituted (1.4.2012) by Education Act 2011 (c. 21), s. 82. (3), Sch. 8 para. 18. (2); S.I. 2012/924, art. 2

F71. S. 46. (1. C) omitted (1.4.2012) by virtue of Education Act 2011 (c. 21), s. 82. (3), Sch. 8 para. 18. (3); S.I. 2012/924, art. 2

F72. Words in s. 46. (1. D) substituted (1.4.2012) by Education Act 2011 (c. 21), s. 82. (3), Sch. 8 para. 18. (4); S.I. 2012/924, art. 2

Commencement Information

I21. S. 46 in force at 20.12.2006 by S.I. 2006/3360, art. 2. (c)

47. Independent schools

(1) In section 157 of the Education Act 2002 (c. 32) (independent school standards) after subsection (1) insert—

"(1. A)In relation to England, the standards do not apply to early years provision for pupils who have not attained the age of three (separate requirements as to such provision being imposed by or under Part 3 of the Childcare Act 2006)."

(2) For subsection (2) of that section substitute—

"(2)In this Chapter "independent school standards" means—

(a) the standards for the time being prescribed under this section, and

(b) in relation to early years provision in England for pupils who have attained the age of three, the Early Years Foundation Stage."

(3) In section 171 of that Act (interpretation of Chapter 1 of Part 10), after the definition of "Chief Inspector" insert—

""early years provision", in relation to England, has the meaning given by section 96. (2) of the Childcare Act 2006;".

Commencement Information

I22. S. 47 in force at 1.9.2008 by S.I. 2008/2261, art. 2 (with Schs. 1, 2)

48. Amendments relating to curriculum

Schedule 1 (which contains amendments relating to the preceding provisions of this Chapter, including amendments excluding or modifying the application to early years provision of provisions of Part 6 of the Education Act 2002 (c. 32)) has effect.

Commencement Information

I23. S. 48 in force at 1.10.2007 for specified purposes by S.I. 2007/2717, art. 2. (d)

I24. S. 48 in force at 1.9.2008 for specified purposes by S.I. 2008/2261, art. 2 (with Schs. 1, 2)

Inspection

49. Inspections

(1) This section applies to early years provision in respect of which the early years provider is registered [F73in the early years register].

(2) The Chief Inspector—

(a) must at such intervals as may be prescribed inspect early years provision to which this section applies,

(b) must inspect early years provision to which this section applies at any time when the Secretary of State requires the Chief Inspector to secure its inspection, and

(c) may inspect early years provision to which this section applies at any other time when the Chief Inspector considers that it would be appropriate for it to be inspected.

(3) Regulations may provide that in prescribed circumstances the Chief Inspector is not required to inspect early years provision at an interval prescribed for the purposes of subsection (2)(a).

(4) Regulations may provide that the Chief Inspector is not required by subsection (2)(a) to inspect early years provision at an [F74independent educational institution] [F75or an alternative provision Academy that is not an independent school] if the early years provision is inspected in prescribed circumstances by a body approved by the Secretary of State for the purposes of this subsection.

(5) A requirement made by the Secretary of State as mentioned in subsection (2)(b) may be imposed in relation to early years provision at particular premises or a class of premises.

[F76. (5. A)The Chief Inspector may charge a prescribed fee for conducting an inspection of early years provision where—

(a) the inspection is conducted at the request of a registered person who provides that early years provision, and

(b) the Chief Inspector is required by the Secretary of State under subsection (2)(b) to conduct that inspection.]

(6) Regulations may make provision requiring the registered person to notify prescribed persons of the fact that early years provision is to be inspected under this section.

(7) If the Chief Inspector so elects in the case of an inspection falling within paragraph (b) or (c) of subsection (2), that inspection is to be treated as if it were an inspection falling within paragraph (a) of that subsection.

Amendments (Textual)

F73. Words in s. 49. (1) substituted (1.4.2014 for specified purposes, 1.9.2014 in so far as not already in force) by Children and Families Act 2014 (c. 6), s. 139. (6), Sch. 4 para. 12; S.I. 2014/889, arts. 3. (m), 7. (e)

F74. Words in s. 49. (4) substituted (5.1.2015) by Education and Skills Act 2008 (c. 25), s. 173. (4), Sch. 1 para. 33; S.I. 2014/3364, art. 2. (z)

F75. Words in s. 49. (4) inserted (1.4.2012) by The Alternative Provision Academies (Consequential Amendments to Acts) (England) Order 2012 (S.I. 2012/976), art. 1, Sch. para. 18 (with art. 3)

F76. S. 49. (5. A) inserted (13.5.2014) by Children and Families Act 2014 (c. 6), ss. 85, 139. (6); S.I. 2014/889, art. 5. (d)

Commencement Information

I25. S. 49 in force at 1.10.2007 for specified purposes by S.I. 2007/2717, art. 2. (c)

I26. S. 49 in force at 1.9.2008 in so far as not already in force by S.I. 2008/2261, art 2 (with Schs. 1, 2)

50. Report of inspections

(1) After conducting an inspection under section 49, the Chief Inspector must make a report in writing on—

(a) the contribution of the early years provision to the well-being of the children for whom it is provided,

(b) the quality and standards of the early years provision,

(c) how far the early years provision meets the needs of the range of children for whom it is provided, and

(d) the quality of leadership and management in connection with the early years provision.

(2) The Chief Inspector—

(a) may send a copy of the report to the Secretary of State and must do so without delay if the Secretary of State requests a copy,

(b) must ensure that a copy of the report is sent without delay to the registered person, 23

(c) must ensure that copies of the report, or such parts of it as he considers appropriate, are sent

to such other persons as may be prescribed, and
(d) may arrange for the report (or parts of it) to be further published in any manner he considers appropriate.
(3) Regulations may make provision—
(a) requiring the registered person to make a copy of any report sent to him under subsection (2)(b) available for inspection by prescribed persons;
(b) requiring the registered person, except in prescribed cases, to provide a copy of the report to prescribed persons;
(c) authorising the registered person in prescribed cases to charge a fee for providing a copy of the report.
F77. (4). . . . .
Amendments (Textual)
F77. S. 50. (4) repealed (1.4.2007) by Education and Inspections Act 2006 (c. 40), s. 188. (3), Sch. 14 para. 111, Sch. 18 Pt. 5; S.I. 2007/935, art. 5. (gg)(ii)
Commencement Information
I27. S. 50 in force at 1.9.2008 in so far as not already in force by S.I. 2008/2261, art. 2 (with Schs. 1, 2)
I28. S. 50. (1)-(3) in force at 1.10.2007 for specified purposes by S.I. 2007/2717, art. 2. (c)

Interpretation

51. Interpretation of Chapter 2.
In this Chapter—
"assessment arrangements" is to be read in accordance with section 41. (2)(c);
"early learning goals" is to be read in accordance with section 41. (2)(a);
"educational programmes" is to be read in accordance with section 41. (2)(b);
"learning and development requirements" means requirements specified by order under section 39. (1)(a);
"welfare requirements" means requirements specified by regulations under section 39. (1)(b).
Commencement Information
I29. S. 51 in force at 1.10.2007 by S.I. 2007/2717, art. 2. (a)

[F78. CHAPTER 2. ARegulation of early years childminder agencies

Amendments (Textual)
F78. Pt. 3 Ch. 2. A inserted (1.4.2014 for specified purposes, 1.9.2014 in so far as not already in force) by Children and Families Act 2014 (c. 6), s. 139. (6), Sch. 4 para. 13; S.I. 2014/889, arts. 3. (m), 7. (e)
51. AApplications for registration
(1) A person may make an application to the Chief Inspector for registration as an early years childminder agency.
(2) An application under subsection (1) must—
(a) give any prescribed information about prescribed matters,
(b) give any other information which the Chief Inspector reasonably requires the applicant to give, and
(c) be accompanied by any prescribed fee.
(3) The Chief Inspector must grant an application under subsection (1) if—
(a) the applicant is not disqualified from registration by regulations under section 76. A, and
(b) it appears to the Chief Inspector that any requirements prescribed for the purposes of this subsection ("the prescribed requirements for registration") are satisfied and are likely to continue

to be satisfied.

(4) The Chief Inspector must refuse any application under subsection (1) which subsection (3) does not require the Chief Inspector to grant.

(5) The prescribed requirements for registration may include requirements relating to—

(a) the applicant;

(b) any persons employed by the applicant;

(c) management and control of the applicant (where the applicant is not an individual);

(d) the provision to the Chief Inspector of information about early years providers registered with the applicant;

(e) the applicant's arrangements for registering early years providers;

(f) the applicant's arrangements in relation to training and monitoring early years providers and providing such persons with information, advice and assistance;

(g) the applicant's arrangements for ensuring that early years provision is of a sufficient standard.

51. B Entry on the register and certificates

(1) If an application under section 51. A is granted, the Chief Inspector must—

(a) register the applicant in the early years register as an early years childminder agency, and

(b) give the applicant a certificate of registration stating that the applicant is so registered.

(2) A certificate of registration given to the applicant in pursuance of subsection (1) must contain prescribed information about prescribed matters.

(3) If there is a change of circumstances which requires the amendment of a certificate of registration, the Chief Inspector must give the early years childminder agency an amended certificate.

(4) If the Chief Inspector is satisfied that a certificate of registration has been lost or destroyed, the Chief Inspector must give the early years childminder agency a copy, on payment by the agency of any prescribed fee.

51. C Conditions on registration

(1) The Chief Inspector may impose such conditions as the Chief Inspector thinks fit on the registration of an early years childminder agency under this Chapter.

(2) The power conferred by subsection (1) may be exercised at the time when the Chief Inspector registers the person in pursuance of section 51. B or at any subsequent time.

(3) The Chief Inspector may at any time vary or remove any condition imposed under subsection (1).

(4) An early years childminder agency commits an offence if, without reasonable excuse, the agency fails to comply with any condition imposed under subsection (1).

(5) A person guilty of an offence under subsection (4) is liable on summary conviction to a fine not exceeding level 5 on the standard scale.

Inspections

51. D Inspections of early years childminder agencies

(1) The Chief Inspector—

(a) must inspect an early years childminder agency at any time when the Secretary of State requires the Chief Inspector to secure its inspection, and

(b) may inspect an early years childminder agency at any other time when the Chief Inspector considers that it would be appropriate for it to be inspected.

(2) For the purposes of an inspection under this section, the Chief Inspector may inspect early years provision provided by early years providers who are registered with the early years childminder agency for the purposes of Chapter 2.

(3) The Chief Inspector may charge a prescribed fee for conducting an inspection of an early years childminder agency where—

(a) the inspection is conducted at the request of the agency, and

(b) the Chief Inspector is required by the Secretary of State under subsection (1)(a) to conduct that inspection.
(4) Regulations may make provision requiring an early years childminder agency to notify prescribed persons of the fact that it is to be inspected under this section.
51. EReports of inspections
(1) After conducting an inspection under section 51. D, the Chief Inspector must make a report in writing on—
  (a) the quality and standards of the services offered by the early years childminder agency to early years providers registered with it,
  (b) the quality of leadership and management in the early years childminder agency, and
  (c) the effectiveness of the arrangements of the early years childminder agency for assuring itself of the quality of the care and education provided by the early years providers registered with it.
(2) The Chief Inspector—
  (a) may send a copy of the report to the Secretary of State and must do so without delay if the Secretary of State requests a copy,
  (b) must ensure that a copy of the report is sent without delay to the early years childminder agency,
  (c) must ensure that copies of the report, or such parts of it as the Chief Inspector considers appropriate, are sent to such other persons as may be prescribed, and
  (d) may arrange for the report (or parts of it) to be further published in any manner the Chief Inspector considers appropriate.
(3) Regulations may make provision—
  (a) requiring the early years childminder agency to make a copy of any report sent to it under subsection (2)(b) available for inspection by prescribed persons;
  (b) requiring the agency, except in prescribed cases, to provide a copy of the report to prescribed persons;
  (c) authorising the agency in prescribed cases to charge a fee for providing a copy of the report.

False representations

51. FFalse representations
(1) A person who without reasonable excuse falsely represents that the person is an early years childminder agency commits an offence.
(2) A person guilty of an offence under subsection (1) is liable on summary conviction to a fine not exceeding level 5 on the standard scale.]

Chapter 3. Regulation of later years provision for children under 8

52. Requirement to register: later years childminders for children under eight
(1) A person may not provide later years childminding in England for a child who has not attained the age of eight unless he is registered [F79as a later years childminder— .
  (a) in Part A of the general childcare register, or
  (b) with a later years childminder agency.]
(2) The Secretary of State may by order provide that, in circumstances specified in the order, subsection (1) does not apply in relation to later years childminding.
(3) The circumstances specified in an order under subsection (2) may relate to one or more of the following matters (among others)—
  (a) the person providing the later years childminding;
  (b) the child or children for whom it is provided;

(c) the nature of the later years childminding;
(d) the premises on which it is provided;
(e) the times during which it is provided;
(f) the arrangements under which it is provided.

(4) If it appears to the Chief Inspector that a person has provided later years childminding in contravention of subsection (1), the Chief Inspector may serve a notice ("an enforcement notice") on the person.

(5) An enforcement notice may be served on a person—
(a) by delivering it to him, or
(b) by sending it by post.

(6) An enforcement notice has effect until it is revoked by the Chief Inspector.

(7) A person commits an offence if, at any time when an enforcement notice has effect in relation to him and without reasonable excuse, he provides later years childminding in contravention of subsection (1).

(8) A person guilty of an offence under subsection (7) is liable on summary conviction to a fine not exceeding level 5 on the standard scale.

Amendments (Textual)
F79. Words in s. 52. (1) substituted (1.4.2014 for specified purposes, 1.9.2014 in so far as not already in force) by Children and Families Act 2014 (c. 6), s. 139. (6), Sch. 4 para. 15; S.I. 2014/889, arts. 3. (m), 7. (e)
Modifications etc. (not altering text)
C3. S. 52. (1) excluded (E.W.) (1.9.2008) by Childcare (Exemptions from Registration) Order 2008 (S.I. 2008/979), arts. 1. (1), 2. (3), 3, 6, 8
Commencement Information
I30. S. 52 in force at 1.10.2007 for specified purposes by S.I. 2007/2717, art. 2. (c)
I31. S. 52 in force at 1.9.2008 in so far as not already in force by S.I. 2008/2261, art. 2 (with Schs. 1, 2)

53. Requirement to register: other later years providers for children under eight

[F80. (1)A person may not provide, for a child who has not attained the age of eight, later years provision on premises in England which are not domestic premises unless the person is registered in Part A of the general childcare register F81....

[F82. (1. ZA)Subsection (1) does not apply in relation to later years provision—
(a) if it is later years childminding in respect of which the person providing it is required to be registered under section 52. (1), or
(b) if it would be later years childminding but for section 96. (9) and in respect of which the person providing it is required to be registered under subsection (1. A).]

(1. A)A person may not provide, for a child who has not attained the age of eight, later years provision F83... in England which would be later years childminding but for section 96. (9) unless the person is registered—
(a) in Part A of the general childcare register F84..., or
(b) with a later years childminder agency F84....]

(2) [F85. Subsections (1) and (1. A) do] not apply in relation to later years provision for a child if—
(a) the provision is made at any of the following [F86institutions] as part of the [F86institution's] activities—
(i) a maintained school,
(ii) a school [F87approved] under section 342 of the Education Act 1996 (c. 56) (approval of non-maintained special schools), or
(iii) [F88an independent educational institution] [F89or an alternative provision Academy that is not an independent school],
(b) the provision is made by the proprietor of the [F90institution] or a person employed to work at the [F90institution], and
[F91. (c)where the provision is made at a school (including a school that is an independent

educational institution)—
(i) the child is a registered pupil at the school, or
(ii) if the provision is made for more than one child, at least one of the children is a registered pupil at the school.]
(3) The Secretary of State may by order provide that, in circumstances specified in the order, [F92subsections (1) and (1. A) do] not apply in relation to later years provision.
(4) The circumstances specified in an order under subsection (3) may relate to one or more of the following matters (among others)—

    (a) the person providing the later years provision;
    (b) the child or children for whom it is provided;
    (c) the nature of the later years provision;
    (d) the premises on which it is provided;
    (e) the times during which it is provided;
    (f) the arrangements under which it is provided.

(5) A person commits an offence if, without reasonable excuse, he provides later years provision in contravention of subsection (1) [F93or (1. A)].
(6) A person guilty of an offence under subsection (5) is liable on summary conviction to a fine not exceeding level 5 on the standard scale.

Amendments (Textual)

F80. S. 53. (1)(1. A) substituted for s. 53. (1) (1.4.2014 for specified purposes, 1.9.2014 in so far as not already in force) by Children and Families Act 2014 (c. 6), s. 139. (6), Sch. 4 para. 16. (2); S.I. 2014/889, arts. 3. (m), 7. (e)

F81. Words in s. 53. (1) omitted (1.1.2016) by virtue of Small Business, Enterprise and Employment Act 2015 (c. 26), s. 164. (1), Sch. 2 para. 6. (a); S.I. 2015/1329, reg. 6. (b)

F82. S. 53. (1. ZA) inserted (1.1.2016) by Small Business, Enterprise and Employment Act 2015 (c. 26), ss. 76. (7)(a), 164. (1); S.I. 2015/1329, reg. 6. (a)

F83. Words in s. 53. (1. A) omitted (1.1.2016) by virtue of Small Business, Enterprise and Employment Act 2015 (c. 26), ss. 76. (7)(b), 164. (1); S.I. 2015/1329, reg. 6. (a)

F84. Words in s. 53. (1. A)(a)(b) omitted (1.1.2016) by virtue of Small Business, Enterprise and Employment Act 2015 (c. 26), s. 164. (1), Sch. 2 para. 6. (b); S.I. 2015/1329, reg. 6. (b)

F85. Words in s. 53. (2) substituted (1.4.2014 for specified purposes, 1.9.2014 in so far as not already in force) by Children and Families Act 2014 (c. 6), s. 139. (6), Sch. 4 para. 16. (3); S.I. 2014/889, arts. 3. (m), 7. (e)

F86. Word in s. 53. (2)(a) substituted (5.1.2015) by Education and Skills Act 2008 (c. 25), s. 173. (4), Sch. 1 para. 34. (2)(a); S.I. 2014/3364, art. 2. (z)

F87. Word in s. 53. (2)(a)(ii) substituted (5.1.2015) by Education and Skills Act 2008 (c. 25), s. 173. (4), Sch. 1 para. 34. (2)(b); S.I. 2014/3364, art. 2. (z)

F88. Words in s. 53. (2)(a)(iii) substituted (5.1.2015) by Education and Skills Act 2008 (c. 25), s. 173. (4), Sch. 1 para. 34. (2)(c); S.I. 2014/3364, art. 2. (z)

F89. Words in s. 53. (2)(a)(iii) inserted (1.4.2012) by The Alternative Provision Academies (Consequential Amendments to Acts) (England) Order 2012 (S.I. 2012/976), art. 1, Sch. para. 19 (with art. 3)

F90. Word in s. 53. (2)(b) substituted (5.1.2015) by Education and Skills Act 2008 (c. 25), s. 173. (4), Sch. 1 para. 34. (3); S.I. 2014/3364, art. 2. (z)

F91. S. 53. (2)(c) substituted (5.1.2015) by Education and Skills Act 2008 (c. 25), s. 173. (4), Sch. 1 para. 34. (4); S.I. 2014/3364, art. 2. (z)

F92. Words in s. 53. (3) substituted (1.4.2014 for specified purposes, 1.9.2014 in so far as not already in force) by Children and Families Act 2014 (c. 6), s. 139. (6), Sch. 4 para. 16. (4); S.I. 2014/889, arts. 3. (m), 7. (e)

F93. Words in s. 53. (5) inserted (1.4.2014 for specified purposes, 1.9.2014 in so far as not already in force) by Children and Families Act 2014 (c. 6), s. 139. (6), Sch. 4 para. 16. (5); S.I. 2014/889, arts. 3. (m), 7. (e)

Modifications etc. (not altering text)

C4. S. 53. (1) excluded (E.W.) (1.9.2008) by Childcare (Exemptions from Registration) Order 2008 (S.I. 2008/979), arts. 1. (1), 2. (4), arts. 4-8
Commencement Information
I32. S. 53 in force at 1.10.2007 for specified purposes by S.I. 2007/2717, art. 2. (c)
I33. S. 53 in force at 1.9.2008 in so far as not already in force by S.I. 2008/2261, art. 2 (with Schs. 1, 2)

Process of registration

54. Applications for registration: later years childminders
(1) A person who proposes to provide later years childminding in respect of which he is required by section 52. (1) to be registered may make an application [F94— .
    (a) to the Chief Inspector for registration as a later years childminder in Part A of the general childcare register, or
    (b) to a later years childminder agency for registration with that agency as a later years childminder.]
(2) An application under subsection (1) must—
    (a) give any prescribed information about prescribed matters,
    (b) give any other information which the Chief Inspector [F95or (as the case may be) the later years childminder agency] reasonably requires the applicant to give, and
    (c) [F96if it is an application to the Chief Inspector,] be accompanied by any prescribed fee.
(3) The Chief Inspector must grant an application under subsection (1) [F97. (a)] if—
    (a) the applicant is not disqualified from registration by regulations under section 75, and
    (b) it appears to the Chief Inspector that any requirements prescribed for the purposes of this subsection ("the prescribed requirements for registration") are satisfied and are likely to continue to be satisfied.
(4) The Chief Inspector must refuse any application under subsection (1) [F98. (a)] which subsection (3) does not require him to grant.
[F99. (4. A)A later years childminder agency may grant an application under subsection (1)(b) only if—
    (a) the applicant is not disqualified from registration by regulations under section 75,
    (b) it appears to the agency that the prescribed requirements for registration are satisfied and are likely to continue to be satisfied, and
    (c) it appears to the agency that any other reasonable requirements it has imposed are satisfied and are likely to continue to be satisfied.]
(5) The prescribed requirements for registration may include requirements relating to—
    (a) the applicant;
    [F100. (aa)prohibiting the applicant from being registered in Part A of the general childcare register as a later years childminder if the applicant is registered with a childminder agency;
    (ab) prohibiting the applicant from being registered with a later years childminder agency as a later years childminder if the applicant is registered—
(i) with another childminder agency;
(ii) in the early years register or the general childcare register;]
    (b) the premises on which the later years childminding is to be provided;
    (c) the arrangements for later years childminding on those premises;
    (d) any person who may be caring for children on those premises;
    (e) any other person who may be on those premises.
Amendments (Textual)
F94. Words in s. 54. (1) substituted (1.4.2014 for specified purposes, 1.9.2014 in so far as not already in force) by Children and Families Act 2014 (c. 6), s. 139. (6), Sch. 4 para. 17. (2); S.I. 2014/889, arts. 3. (m), 7. (e)
F95. Words in s. 54. (2)(b) inserted (1.4.2014 for specified purposes, 1.9.2014 in so far as not

already in force) by Children and Families Act 2014 (c. 6), s. 139. (6), Sch. 4 para. 17. (3)(a); S.I. 2014/889, arts. 3. (m), 7. (e)
F96. Words in s. 54. (2)(c) inserted (1.4.2014 for specified purposes, 1.9.2014 in so far as not already in force) by Children and Families Act 2014 (c. 6), s. 139. (6), Sch. 4 para. 17. (3)(b); S.I. 2014/889, arts. 3. (m), 7. (e)
F97. Word in s. 54. (3) inserted (1.4.2014 for specified purposes, 1.9.2014 in so far as not already in force) by Children and Families Act 2014 (c. 6), s. 139. (6), Sch. 4 para. 17. (4); S.I. 2014/889, arts. 3. (m), 7. (e)
F98. Word in s. 54. (4) inserted (1.4.2014 for specified purposes, 1.9.2014 in so far as not already in force) by Children and Families Act 2014 (c. 6), s. 139. (6), Sch. 4 para. 17. (4); S.I. 2014/889, arts. 3. (m), 7. (e)
F99. S. 54. (4. A) inserted (1.4.2014 for specified purposes, 1.9.2014 in so far as not already in force) by Children and Families Act 2014 (c. 6), s. 139. (6), Sch. 4 para. 17. (5); S.I. 2014/889, arts. 3. (m), 7. (e)
F100. S. 54. (5)(aa)(ab) inserted (1.4.2014 for specified purposes, 1.9.2014 in so far as not already in force) by Children and Families Act 2014 (c. 6), s. 139. (6), Sch. 4 para. 17. (6); S.I. 2014/889, arts. 3. (m), 7. (e)
Commencement Information
I34. S. 54 in force at 1.10.2007 for specified purposes by S.I. 2007/2717, art. 2. (c)
I35. S. 54 in force at 1.9.2008 in so far as not already in force by S.I. 2008/2261, art. 2 (with Schs. 1, 2)
55. Applications for registration: other later years providers
(1) A person who proposes to provide F101... later years provision in respect of which he is required by section 53. (1) to be registered may make an application to the Chief Inspector for registration as a later years provider F101....
[F102. (1. A)A person who proposes to provide F103... later years provision in respect of which the person is required by section 53. (1. A) to be registered may make an application—
    (a) to the Chief Inspector for registration as a later years provider F104..., or
    (b) to a later years childminder agency for registration with that agency as a later years provider F104....]
(2) An application under subsection (1) [F105or (1. A)] must—
    (a) give any prescribed information about prescribed matters,
    (b) give any other information which the Chief Inspector [F106or (as the case may be) the later years childminder agency] reasonably requires the applicant to give, and
    (c) [F107if it is an application to the Chief Inspector,] be accompanied by any prescribed fee.
(3) The Chief Inspector must grant an application under subsection (1) [F108or (1. A)(a)] if—
    (a) the applicant is not disqualified from registration by regulations under section 75, and
    (b) it appears to the Chief Inspector that any requirements prescribed for the purposes of this subsection ("the prescribed requirements for registration") are satisfied and are likely to continue to be satisfied.
(4) The Chief Inspector must refuse any application under subsection (1) [F109or (1. A)(a)] which subsection (3) does not require him to grant.
[F110. (4. A)A later years childminder agency may grant an application under subsection (1. A)(b) only if—
    (a) the applicant is not disqualified from registration by regulations under section 75,
    (b) it appears to the agency that the prescribed requirements for registration are satisfied and are likely to continue to be satisfied, and
    (c) it appears to the agency that any other reasonable requirements it has imposed are satisfied and are likely to continue to be satisfied.]
(5) The prescribed requirements for registration may include requirements relating to—
    (a) the applicant;
[F111. (aa)prohibiting the applicant from being registered in Part A of the general childcare register as a later years provider other than a childminder if the applicant is registered with a

childminder agency;

(ab) prohibiting the applicant from being registered with a later years childminder agency as a later years provider other than a childminder if the applicant is registered—

(i) with another childminder agency;

(ii) in the early years register or the general childcare register;]

(b) the premises on which the later years provision is to be provided;

(c) the arrangements for later years provision on those premises;

(d) any person who may be caring for children on those premises;

(e) any other person who may be on those premises.

Amendments (Textual)

F101. Words in s. 55. (1) omitted (1.1.2016) by virtue of Small Business, Enterprise and Employment Act 2015 (c. 26), s. 164. (1), Sch. 2 para. 7. (a); S.I. 2015/1329, reg. 6. (b)

F102. S. 55. (1. A) inserted (1.4.2014 for specified purposes, 1.9.2014 in so far as not already in force) by Children and Families Act 2014 (c. 6), s. 139. (6), Sch. 4 para. 18. (2); S.I. 2014/889, arts. 3. (m), 7. (e)

F103. Words in s. 55. (1. A) omitted (1.1.2016) by virtue of Small Business, Enterprise and Employment Act 2015 (c. 26), s. 164. (1), Sch. 2 para. 7. (b); S.I. 2015/1329, reg. 6. (b)

F104. Words in s. 55. (1. A)(a)(b) omitted (1.1.2016) by virtue of Small Business, Enterprise and Employment Act 2015 (c. 26), s. 164. (1), Sch. 2 para. 7. (c); S.I. 2015/1329, reg. 6. (b)

F105. Words in s. 55. (2) inserted (1.4.2014 for specified purposes, 1.9.2014 in so far as not already in force) by Children and Families Act 2014 (c. 6), s. 139. (6), Sch. 4 para. 18. (3)(a); S.I. 2014/889, arts. 3. (m), 7. (e)

F106. Words in s. 55. (2)(b) inserted (1.4.2014 for specified purposes, 1.9.2014 in so far as not already in force) by Children and Families Act 2014 (c. 6), s. 139. (6), Sch. 4 para. 18. (3)(b); S.I. 2014/889, arts. 3. (m), 7. (e)

F107. Words in s. 55. (2)(c) inserted (1.4.2014 for specified purposes, 1.9.2014 in so far as not already in force) by Children and Families Act 2014 (c. 6), s. 139. (6), Sch. 4 para. 18. (3)(c); S.I. 2014/889, arts. 3. (m), 7. (e)

F108. Words in s. 55. (3) inserted (1.4.2014 for specified purposes, 1.9.2014 in so far as not already in force) by Children and Families Act 2014 (c. 6), s. 139. (6), Sch. 4 para. 18. (4); S.I. 2014/889, arts. 3. (m), 7. (e)

F109. Words in s. 55. (4) inserted (1.4.2014 for specified purposes, 1.9.2014 in so far as not already in force) by Children and Families Act 2014 (c. 6), s. 139. (6), Sch. 4 para. 18. (4); S.I. 2014/889, arts. 3. (m), 7. (e)

F110. S. 55. (4. A) inserted (1.4.2014 for specified purposes, 1.9.2014 in so far as not already in force) by Children and Families Act 2014 (c. 6), s. 139. (6), Sch. 4 para. 18. (5); S.I. 2014/889, arts. 3. (m), 7. (e)

F111. S. 55. (5)(aa)(ab) inserted (1.4.2014 for specified purposes, 1.9.2014 in so far as not already in force) by Children and Families Act 2014 (c. 6), s. 139. (6), Sch. 4 para. 18. (6); S.I. 2014/889, arts. 3. (m), 7. (e)

Commencement Information

I36. S. 55 in force at 1.10.2007 for specified purposes by S.I. 2007/2717, art. 2. (c)

I37. S. 55 in force at 1.9.2008 in so far as not already in force by S.I. 2008/2261, art. 2 (with Schs. 1, 2)

56. Entry on the register and certificates

(1) If an application under section 54. (1) [F112. (a)] is granted, the Chief Inspector must—

(a) register the applicant in Part A of the general childcare register as a later years childminder, and

(b) give the applicant a certificate of registration stating that he is so registered.

(2) If an application under section 55. (1) [F113or (1. A)(a)] is granted, the Chief Inspector must—

(a) register the applicant in Part A of the general childcare register as a later years provider other than a childminder F114..., and

(b) give the applicant a certificate of registration stating that he is so registered.

(3) A certificate of registration given to the applicant in pursuance of subsection (1) or (2) must contain prescribed information about prescribed matters.
(4) If there is a change of circumstances which requires the amendment of a certificate of registration, the Chief Inspector must give the registered later years provider an amended certificate.
(5) If the Chief Inspector is satisfied that a certificate of registration has been lost or destroyed, the Chief Inspector must give the registered later years provider a copy, on payment by the provider of any prescribed fee.

Amendments (Textual)
F112. Word in s. 56. (1) inserted (1.4.2014 for specified purposes, 1.9.2014 in so far as not already in force) by Children and Families Act 2014 (c. 6), s. 139. (6), Sch. 4 para. 19. (2); S.I. 2014/889, arts. 3. (m), 7. (e)
F113. Words in s. 56. (2) inserted (1.4.2014 for specified purposes, 1.9.2014 in so far as not already in force) by Children and Families Act 2014 (c. 6), s. 139. (6), Sch. 4 para. 19. (3); S.I. 2014/889, arts. 3. (m), 7. (e)
F114. Words in s. 56. (2)(a) omitted (1.1.2016) by virtue of Small Business, Enterprise and Employment Act 2015 (c. 26), s. 164. (1), Sch. 2 para. 8; S.I. 2015/1329, reg. 6. (b)

Commencement Information
I38. S. 56 in force at 1.10.2007 for specified purposes by S.I. 2007/2717, art. 2. (c)
I39. S. 56 in force at 1.9.2008 in so far as not already in force by S.I. 2008/2261, art. 2 (with Schs. 1, 2)

[F115 56. A Later years childminder agencies: registers and certificates
(1) If an application under section 54. (1)(b) is granted, the later years childminder agency must—
    (a) register the applicant in the register maintained by the agency as a later years childminder, and
    (b) give the applicant a certificate of registration stating that he or she is so registered.
(2) If an application under section 55. (1. A)(b) is granted, the later years childminder agency must—
    (a) register the applicant in the register maintained by the agency as a later years provider other than a childminder F116..., and
    (b) give the applicant a certificate of registration stating that he or she is so registered.
(3) A certificate of registration given to the applicant in pursuance of subsection (1) or (2) must contain prescribed information about prescribed matters.
(4) If there is a change of circumstances which requires the amendment of a certificate of registration, the later years childminder agency must give the registered later years provider an amended certificate.]

Amendments (Textual)
F115. S. 56. A inserted (1.4.2014 for specified purposes, 1.9.2014 in so far as not already in force) by Children and Families Act 2014 (c. 6), s. 139. (6), Sch. 4 para. 20; S.I. 2014/889, arts. 3. (m), 7. (e)
F116. Words in s. 56. A(2)(a) omitted (1.1.2016) by virtue of Small Business, Enterprise and Employment Act 2015 (c. 26), s. 164. (1), Sch. 2 para. 9; S.I. 2015/1329, reg. 6. (b)

F117 57. Special procedure for providers registered in the early years register
(1) If a person who is registered in the early years register as an early years childminder gives notice to the Chief Inspector that he proposes to provide later years childminding in respect of which he is required to be registered under this Chapter, the Chief Inspector must—
    (a) register the person in Part A of the general childcare register as a later years childminder, and
    (b) give the person a certificate of registration stating that he is so registered.
(2) If a person who is registered in the early years register F118... as an early years provider other than a childminder gives notice to the Chief Inspector that he proposes to provide later years provision in respect of which he is required to be registered under this Chapter F118..., the Chief Inspector must—

(a) register the person in Part A of the general childcare register as a later years provider other than a childminder F118..., and
   (b) give the person a certificate of registration stating that he is so registered.
(3) Subsections (3) to (5) of section 56 apply in relation to a certificate of registration given in pursuance of subsection (1) or (2) of this section as they apply in relation to a certificate of registration given in pursuance of subsection (1) or (2) of that section.
Amendments (Textual)
F117. Words in s. 57 substituted (1.4.2014 for specified purposes, 1.9.2014 in so far as not already in force) by Children and Families Act 2014 (c. 6), s. 139. (6), Sch. 4 para. 21; S.I. 2014/889, arts. 3. (m), 7. (e)
F118. Words in s. 57. (2) omitted (1.1.2016) by virtue of Small Business, Enterprise and Employment Act 2015 (c. 26), s. 164. (1), Sch. 2 para. 10; S.I. 2015/1329, reg. 6. (b)
Commencement Information
I40. S. 57 in force at 1.9.2008 by S.I. 2008/2261, art. 2 (with Schs. 1, 2)
[F11957. ASpecial procedure for providers registered with early years childminder agencies
(1) Subsection (2) applies where—
   (a) a person is registered with an early years childminder agency as an early years childminder, and
   (b) that agency is also a later years childminder agency.
(2) If the person gives notice to the agency that he or she proposes to provide later years childminding in respect of which he or she is required to be registered under this Chapter, the agency must—
   (a) register the person in the register maintained by the agency as a later years childminder, and
   (b) give the person a certificate of registration stating that he or she is so registered.
(3) Subsection (4) applies where—
   (a) a person is registered with an early years childminder agency F120... as an early years provider other than a childminder, and
   (b) that agency is also a later years childminder agency.
(4) If the person gives notice to the agency that he or she proposes to provide later years provision in respect of which he or she is required to be registered under this Chapter F121..., the agency must—
   (a) register the person in the register maintained by the agency as a later years provider other than a childminder F121..., and
   (b) give the person a certificate of registration stating that he or she is so registered.
(5) Subsections (3) and (4) of section 56. A apply in relation to a certificate of registration given in pursuance of subsection (2) or (4) of this section as they apply in relation to a certificate of registration given in pursuance of subsection (1) or (2) of that section.]
Amendments (Textual)
F119. S. 57. A inserted (1.4.2014 for specified purposes, 1.9.2014 in so far as not already in force) by Children and Families Act 2014 (c. 6), s. 139. (6), Sch. 4 para. 22; S.I. 2014/889, arts. 3. (m), 7. (e)
F120. Words in s. 57. A(3) omitted (1.1.2016) by virtue of Small Business, Enterprise and Employment Act 2015 (c. 26), s. 164. (1), Sch. 2 para. 11. (a); S.I. 2015/1329, reg. 6. (b)
F121. Words in s. 57. A(4) omitted (1.1.2016) by virtue of Small Business, Enterprise and Employment Act 2015 (c. 26), s. 164. (1), Sch. 2 para. 11. (b); S.I. 2015/1329, reg. 6. (b)

Regulation

58. Conditions on registration
(1) The Chief Inspector may impose such conditions as he thinks fit on the registration of a later years provider [F122in Part A of the general childcare register].
(2) The power conferred by subsection (1) may be exercised at the time when the Chief Inspector

registers the person in pursuance of section 56 or 57 or at any subsequent time.
(3) The Chief Inspector may at any time vary or remove any condition imposed under subsection (1).
(4) The power conferred by subsection (1) includes power to impose conditions for the purpose of giving effect to regulations under section 59.
(5) A later years provider registered [F123in Part A of the general childcare register] commits an offence if, without reasonable excuse, he fails to comply with any condition imposed under subsection (1).
(6) A person guilty of an offence under subsection (5) is liable on summary conviction to a fine not exceeding level 5 on the standard scale.

Amendments (Textual)
F122. Words in s. 58. (1) substituted (1.4.2014 for specified purposes, 1.9.2014 in so far as not already in force) by Children and Families Act 2014 (c. 6), s. 139. (6), Sch. 4 para. 23; S.I. 2014/889, arts. 3. (m), 7. (e)
F123. Words in s. 58. (5) substituted (1.4.2014 for specified purposes) by Children and Families Act 2014 (c. 6), s. 139. (6), Sch. 4 para. 23; S.I. 2014/889, art. 3. (m)

Commencement Information
I41. S. 58 in force at 1.9.2008 by S.I. 2008/2261, art. 2 (with Schs. 1, 2)

59. Regulations governing activities

(1) This section applies to—
    (a) later years providers providing later years provision in respect of which they are registered under this Chapter, and
    (b) later years providers providing later years provision in respect of which, but for section 53. (2) (exemption for provision for children at certain schools), they would be required to be registered under this Chapter.
(2) The Secretary of State may, after consulting the Chief Inspector and any other person he considers appropriate, make regulations governing the activities of later years providers to whom this section applies.
(3) The regulations may deal with the following matters (among others)—
    (a) the welfare of the children concerned;
    (b) the arrangements for safeguarding the children concerned;
    (c) suitability of persons to care for, or be in regular contact with, the children concerned;
    (d) qualifications and training;
    (e) the suitability of premises and equipment;
    (f) the manner in which the later years provision is organised;
    (g) procedures for dealing with complaints;
    (h) the keeping of records;
    (i) the provision of information.
(4) The power to make regulations under this section may be exercised so as confer powers or impose duties on the Chief Inspector [F124or later years childminder agencies] in the exercise of F125... functions under this Part.
(5) In particular, it may be so exercised so as to require the Chief Inspector [F126or later years childminder agencies], in exercising F127... functions under this Part, to have regard to factors, standards and other matters prescribed by or referred to in the regulations.
(6) If the regulations require any person (other than the Chief Inspector) to have regard to or to meet factors, standards and other matters prescribed by or referred to in the regulations, they may also provide for any allegation that the person has failed to do so to be taken into account—
    (a) by the Chief Inspector in the exercise of his functions under this Part,
    [F128. (aa)by later years childminder agencies in the exercise of functions under this Part,] or
    (b) in any proceedings under this Part.
(7) The regulations may provide—
    (a) that a person who without reasonable excuse fails to comply with any requirement of the regulations is guilty of an offence, and

(b) that a person guilty of the offence is liable on summary conviction to a fine not exceeding level 5 on the standard scale.

Amendments (Textual)

F124. Words in s. 59. (4) inserted (1.4.2014 for specified purposes, 1.9.2014 in so far as not already in force) by Children and Families Act 2014 (c. 6), s. 139. (6), Sch. 4 para. 24. (2)(a); S.I. 2014/889, arts. 3. (m), 7. (e)

F125. Word in s. 59. (4) omiited (1.4.2014 for specified purposes, 1.9.2014 in so far as not already in force) by Children and Families Act 2014 (c. 6), s. 139. (6), Sch. 4 para. 24. (2)(b); S.I. 2014/889, arts. 3. (m), 7. (e)

F126. Words in s. 59. (5) inserted (1.4.2014 for specified purposes, 1.9.2014 in so far as not already in force) by Children and Families Act 2014 (c. 6), s. 139. (6), Sch. 4 para. 24. (3)(a); S.I. 2014/889, arts. 3. (m), 7. (e)

F127. Word in s. 59. (5) omitted (1.4.2014 for specified purposes, 1.9.2014 in so far as not already in force) by virtue of Children and Families Act 2014 (c. 6), s. 139. (6), Sch. 4 para. 24. (3)(b); S.I. 2014/889, arts. 3. (m), 7. (e)

F128. S. 59. (6)(aa) inserted (1.4.2014 for specified purposes, 1.9.2014 in so far as not already in force) by Children and Families Act 2014 (c. 6), s. 139. (6), Sch. 4 para. 24. (4); S.I. 2014/889, arts. 3. (m), 7. (e)

Commencement Information

I42. S. 59 in force at 1.10.2007 for specified purposes by S.I. 2007/2717, art. 2. (c)

I43. S. 59 in force at 1.9.2008 in so far as not already in force by S.I. 2008/2261, art. 2 (with Schs. 1, 2)

Inspection

60. Inspections

(1) This section applies to later years provision in respect of which the provider is registered [F129in Part A of the general childcare register].

(2) The Chief Inspector—

(a) must inspect later years provision to which this section applies at any time when the Secretary of State requires the Chief Inspector to secure its inspection, and

(b) may inspect later years provision to which this section applies at any other time when the Chief Inspector considers that it would be appropriate for it to be inspected.

(3) A requirement made by the Secretary of State as mentioned in subsection (2)(a) may be imposed in relation to later years provision at particular premises or a class of premises.

(4) Regulations may make provision requiring the registered person to notify prescribed persons of the fact that later years provision is to be inspected under this section.

Amendments (Textual)

F129. Words in s. 60. (1) substituted (1.4.2014 for specified purposes, 1.9.2014 in so far as not already in force) by Children and Families Act 2014 (c. 6), s. 139. (6), Sch. 4 para. 25; S.I. 2014/889, arts. 3. (m), 7. (e)

Commencement Information

I44. S. 60 in force at 1.10.2007 for specified purposes by S.I. 2007/2717, art. 2. (c)

I45. S. 60 in force at 1.9.2008 in so far as not already in force by S.I. 2008/2261, art. 2 (with Schs. 1, 2)

61. Report of inspections

(1) After conducting an inspection under section 60, the Chief Inspector may make a report in writing on such of the following matters as he considers appropriate—

(a) the contribution of the later years provision to the well-being of the children for whom it is provided,

(b) the quality and standards of the later years provision,

(c) how far the later years provision meets the needs of the range of children for whom it is

provided, and
(d) the quality of leadership and management in connection with the later years provision.
(2) The Chief Inspector—
(a) may send a copy of the report to the Secretary of State and must do so without delay if the Secretary of State requests a copy,
(b) must ensure that a copy of the report is sent without delay to the registered person,
(c) must ensure that copies of the report, or such parts of it as he considers appropriate, are sent to such other persons as may be prescribed, and
(d) may arrange for the report (or parts of it) to be further published in any manner he considers appropriate.
(3) Regulations may make provision—
(a) requiring the registered person to make a copy of any report sent to him under subsection (2)(b) available for inspection by prescribed persons;
(b) requiring the registered person, except in prescribed cases, to provide a copy of the report to prescribed persons;
(c) authorising the registered person in prescribed cases to charge a fee for providing a copy of the report.
F130. (4)............................
Amendments (Textual)
F130. S. 61. (4) repealed (1.4.2007) by Education and Inspections Act 2006 (c. 40), s. 188. (3), Sch. 14 para. 112, Sch. 18 Pt. 5; S.I. 2007/935, art. 5. (gg)(ii)
Commencement Information
I46. S. 61 in force at 1.10.2007 for specified purposes by S.I. 2007/2717, art. 2. (c)
I47. S. 61. (1)-(3) in force at 1.9.2008 in so far as not already in force by S.I. 2008/2261, art. 2 (with Schs. 1, 2)

[F131. CHAPTER 3. ARegulation of later years childminder agencies

Amendments (Textual)
F131. Pt. 3 Ch. 3. A inserted (1.4.2014 for specified purposes, 1.9.2014 in so far as not already in force) by Children and Families Act 2014 (c. 6), s. 139. (6), Sch. 4 para. 26; S.I. 2014/889, arts. 3. (m), 7. (e)
61. AApplications for registration
(1) A person may make an application to the Chief Inspector for registration as a later years childminder agency.
(2) An application under subsection (1) must—
(a) give any prescribed information about prescribed matters,
(b) give any other information which the Chief Inspector reasonably requires the applicant to give, and
(c) be accompanied by any prescribed fee.
(3) The Chief Inspector must grant an application under subsection (1) if—
(a) the applicant is not disqualified from registration by regulations under section 76. A, and
(b) it appears to the Chief Inspector that any requirements prescribed for the purposes of this subsection ("the prescribed requirements for registration") are satisfied and are likely to continue to be satisfied.
(4) The Chief Inspector must refuse any application under subsection (1) which subsection (3) does not require the Chief Inspector to grant.
(5) The prescribed requirements for registration may include requirements relating to—
(a) the applicant;
(b) any persons employed by the applicant;
(c) management and control of the applicant (where the applicant is not an individual);

    (d) the provision to the Chief Inspector of information about later years providers registered with the applicant;
    (e) the applicant's arrangements for registering later years providers;
    (f) the applicant's arrangements in relation to training and monitoring later years providers, and providing such persons with information, advice and assistance;
    (g) the applicant's arrangements for ensuring that later years provision is of a sufficient standard.

61. BEntry on the register and certificates

(1) If an application under section 61. A is granted, the Chief Inspector must—
    (a) register the applicant in Part A of the general childcare register as a later years childminder agency, and
    (b) give the applicant a certificate of registration stating that the applicant is so registered.
(2) A certificate of registration given to the applicant in pursuance of subsection (1) must contain prescribed information about prescribed matters.
(3) If there is a change of circumstances which requires the amendment of a certificate of registration, the Chief Inspector must give the later years childminder agency an amended certificate.
(4) If the Chief Inspector is satisfied that a certificate of registration has been lost or destroyed, the Chief Inspector must give the later years childminder agency a copy, on payment by the agency of any prescribed fee.

61. CSpecial procedure for registered early years childminder agencies

(1) If an early years childminder agency gives notice to the Chief Inspector of a wish to be a later years childminder agency the Chief Inspector must—
    (a) register the early years childminder agency in Part A of the general childcare register as a later years childminder agency, and
    (b) give the agency a certificate of registration stating that it is so registered.
(2) Subsections (2) to (4) of section 61. B apply in relation to a certificate of registration given in pursuance of subsection (1) of this section as they apply in relation to a certificate of registration given in pursuance of subsection (1) of that section.

61. DConditions on registration

(1) The Chief Inspector may impose such conditions as the Chief Inspector thinks fit on the registration of a later years childminder agency under this Chapter.
(2) The power conferred by subsection (1) may be exercised at the time when the Chief Inspector registers the person in pursuance of section 61. B or 61. C or at any subsequent time.
(3) The Chief Inspector may at any time vary or remove any condition imposed under subsection (1).
(4) A later years childminder agency commits an offence if, without reasonable excuse, the agency fails to comply with any condition imposed under subsection (1).
(5) A person guilty of an offence under subsection (4) is liable on summary conviction to a fine not exceeding level 5 on the standard scale.

Inspections

61. EInspections of later years childminder agencies

(1) The Chief Inspector—
    (a) must inspect a later years childminder agency at any time when the Secretary of State requires the Chief Inspector to secure its inspection, and
    (b) may inspect a later years childminder agency at any other time when the Chief Inspector considers that it would be appropriate for it to be inspected.
(2) For the purposes of an inspection under this section, the Chief Inspector may inspect later years provision provided by later years providers who are registered with the later years childminder agency for the purposes of Chapter 3.

(3) The Chief Inspector may charge a prescribed fee for conducting an inspection of a later years childminder agency where—
   (a) the inspection is conducted at the request of the agency, and
   (b) the Chief Inspector is required by the Secretary of State under subsection (1)(a) to conduct that inspection.
(4) Regulations may make provision requiring a later years childminder agency to notify prescribed persons of the fact that it is to be inspected under this section.

61. FReports of inspections
(1) After conducting an inspection under section 61. E, the Chief Inspector must make a report in writing on—
   (a) the quality and standards of the services offered by the later years childminder agency to later years providers registered with it,
   (b) the quality of leadership and management in the later years childminder agency, and
   (c) the effectiveness of the arrangements of the later years childminder agency for assuring itself of the quality of the care and education provided by the later years providers registered with it.
(2) The Chief Inspector—
   (a) may send a copy of the report to the Secretary of State and must do so without delay if the Secretary of State requests a copy,
   (b) must ensure that a copy of the report is sent without delay to the later years childminder agency,
   (c) must ensure that copies of the report, or such parts of it as the Chief Inspector considers appropriate, are sent to such other persons as may be prescribed, and
   (d) may arrange for the report (or parts of it) to be further published in any manner the Chief Inspector considers appropriate.
(3) Regulations may make provision—
   (a) requiring the later years childminder agency to make a copy of any report sent to it under subsection (2)(b) available for inspection by prescribed persons;
   (b) requiring the agency, except in prescribed cases, to provide a copy of the report to prescribed persons;
   (c) authorising the agency in prescribed cases to charge a fee for providing a copy of the report.

False representations

61. GFalse representations
(1) A person who without reasonable excuse falsely represents that the person is a later years childminder agency commits an offence.
(2) A person guilty of an offence under subsection (1) is liable on summary conviction to a fine not exceeding level 5 on the standard scale.]

Chapter 4. Voluntary registration

62. Applications for registration on the general register: childminders
(1) A person who provides or proposes to provide in England—
   (a) later years childminding for a child who has attained the age of eight, or
   (b) early years childminding or later years childminding for a child who has not attained that age but in respect of which the person is not required to be registered under Chapter 2 or 3,
may make an application to the Chief Inspector for registration in Part B of the general childcare register as a childminder.
(2) An application under subsection (1) must—
   (a) give any prescribed information about prescribed matters,
   (b) give any other information which the Chief Inspector reasonably requires the applicant to give, and

(c) be accompanied by any prescribed fee.

(3) The Chief Inspector must grant an application under subsection (1) if—

(a) the applicant is not disqualified from registration by regulations under section 75, and

(b) it appears to the Chief Inspector that any requirements prescribed for the purposes of this subsection ("the prescribed requirements for registration") are satisfied and are likely to continue to be satisfied.

(4) The Chief Inspector must refuse any application under subsection (1) which subsection (3) does not require him to grant.

(5) The prescribed requirements for registration may include requirements relating to—

(a) the applicant;

(b) the premises on which the childminding is being (or is to be) provided;

(c) the arrangements for childminding on those premises;

(d) any person who may be caring for children on those premises;

(e) any other person who may be on those premises.

Commencement Information

I48. S. 62 in force at 20.12.2006 for specified purposes by S.I. 2006/3360, art. 2. (d)

I49. S. 62. (1)(a)(2)-(5) in force at 6.4.2007 in so far as not already in force by S.I. 2007/1019, art. 4 (with art. 6, Sch. para. 2)

I50. S. 62. (1)(b) in force at 1.9.2008 in so far as not already in force by S.I. 2008/2261, art. 2 (with Schs. 1, 2)

63. Applications for registration on the general register: other childcare providers

(1) A person who provides or proposes to provide on premises in England—

(a) later years provision (other than later years childminding) for a child who has attained the age of eight, or

(b) early years provision or later years provision (other than early years or later years childminding) for a child who has not attained that age but in respect of which the person is not required to be registered under Chapter 2 or 3,

may make an application to the Chief Inspector for registration in Part B of the general childcare register F132....

(2) An application under subsection (1) must—

(a) give any prescribed information about prescribed matters;

(b) give any other information which the Chief Inspector reasonably requires the applicant to give;

(c) be accompanied by any prescribed fee.

(3) An application under subsection (1) may not be made in respect of provision for a child who has attained the age of [F133two] if—

(a) the provision is made at any of the following [F134institutions] as part of the [F134institution's] activities—

(i) a maintained school,

(ii) a school [F135approved] under section 342 of the Education Act 1996 (c. 56) (approval of non-maintained special schools), or

(iii) [F136an independent educational institution][F137or an alternative provision Academy that is not an independent school],

(b) the provision is made by the proprietor of the [F138institution] or a person employed to work at the [F138institution], and

[F139. (c)where the provision is made at a school (including a school that is an independent educational institution)—

(i) the child is a registered pupil at the school, or

(ii) if the provision is made for more than one child, at least one of the children is a registered pupil at the school.]

(4) The Chief Inspector must grant an application under subsection (1) if—

(a) the applicant is not disqualified from registration by regulations under section 75, and

(b) it appears to the Chief Inspector that any requirements prescribed for the purposes of this subsection ("the prescribed requirements for registration") are satisfied and are likely to continue to be satisfied.

(5) The Chief Inspector must refuse any application under subsection (1) which subsection (4) does not require him to grant.

(6) The prescribed requirements for registration may include requirements relating to—
   (a) the applicant;
   (b) the premises on which the childcare is being (or is to be) provided;
   (c) the arrangements for childcare on those premises;
   (d) any person who may be caring for children on those premises;
   (e) any other person who may be on those premises.

Amendments (Textual)

F132. Words in s. 63. (1) omitted (1.1.2016) by virtue of Small Business, Enterprise and Employment Act 2015 (c. 26), s. 164. (1), Sch. 2 para. 12; S.I. 2015/1329, reg. 6. (b)

F133. Word in s. 63. (3) substituted (26.5.2015) by Small Business, Enterprise and Employment Act 2015 (c. 26), ss. 75. (3)(a), 164. (3)(e)

F134. Word in s. 63. (3)(a) substituted (5.1.2015) by Education and Skills Act 2008 (c. 25), s. 173. (4), Sch. 1 para. 35. (2)(a); S.I. 2014/3364, art. 2. (z)

F135. Word in s. 63. (3)(a)(ii) substituted (5.1.2015) by Education and Skills Act 2008 (c. 25), s. 173. (4), Sch. 1 para. 35. (2)(b); S.I. 2014/3364, art. 2. (z)

F136. Words in s. 63. (3)(a)(iii) substituted (5.1.2015) by Education and Skills Act 2008 (c. 25), s. 173. (4), Sch. 1 para. 35. (2)(c); S.I. 2014/3364, art. 2. (z)

F137. Words in s. 63. (3)(a)(iii) inserted (1.4.2012) by The Alternative Provision Academies (Consequential Amendments to Acts) (England) Order 2012 (S.I. 2012/976), art. 1, Sch. para. 20 (with art. 3)

F138. Word in s. 63. (3)(b) substituted (5.1.2015) by Education and Skills Act 2008 (c. 25), s. 173. (4), Sch. 1 para. 35. (3); S.I. 2014/3364, art. 2. (z)

F139. S. 63. (3)(c) substituted (5.1.2015) by Education and Skills Act 2008 (c. 25), s. 173. (4), Sch. 1 para. 35. (4); S.I. 2014/3364, art. 2. (z)

Commencement Information

I51. S. 63 in force at 20.12.2006 for specified purposes by S.I. 2006/3360, art. 2. (d)

I52. S. 63. (1)(a)(2)-(6) in force at 6.4.2007 in so far as not already in force by S.I. 2007/1019, art. 4 (with art. 6, Sch. para. 3)

I53. S. 63. (1)(b) in force at 1.9.2008 in so far as not already in force by S.I. 2008/2261, art. 2 (with Schs. 1, 2)

64. Entry on the register and certificates

(1) If an application under section 62. (1) is granted, the Chief Inspector must—
   (a) register the applicant in Part B of the general childcare register as a childminder, and
   (b) give the applicant a certificate of registration stating that he is so registered.

(2) If an application under section 63. (1) is granted, the Chief Inspector must—
   (a) register the applicant in Part B of the general childcare register as a provider of childcare other than a childminder F140..., and
   (b) give the applicant a certificate of registration stating that he is so registered.

(3) A certificate of registration given to the applicant in pursuance of subsection (1) or (2) must contain prescribed information about prescribed matters.

(4) If there is a change of circumstances which requires the amendment of a certificate of registration, the Chief Inspector must give the registered person an amended certificate.

(5) If the Chief Inspector is satisfied that a certificate of registration has been lost or destroyed, the Chief Inspector must give the registered person a copy, on payment by the provider of any prescribed fee.

Amendments (Textual)

F140. Words in s. 64. (2) omitted (1.1.2016) by virtue of Small Business, Enterprise and Employment Act 2015 (c. 26), s. 164. (1), Sch. 2 para. 13; S.I. 2015/1329, reg. 6. (b)

Commencement Information

I54. S. 64 in force at 20.12.2006 for specified purposes by S.I. 2006/3360, art. 2. (d)
I55. S. 64 in force at 6.4.2007 in so far as not already in force by S.I. 2007/1019, art. 4

65. Special procedure for persons already registered [F141 in a childcare register]

(1) If a person who is registered as a childminder in the early years register or in Part A of the general childcare register gives notice to the Chief Inspector that he wishes to be registered in Part B of the general childcare register, the Chief Inspector must—

(a) register the person in Part B of the general childcare register as a childminder, and
(b) give the applicant a certificate of registration stating that he is so registered.

(2) If a person who is registered (otherwise than as a childminder) in the early years register or in Part A of the general childcare register F142... gives notice to the Chief Inspector that he wishes to be registered in Part B of the general childcare register F142..., the Chief Inspector must—

(a) register the person in Part B of the general childcare register as a provider of childcare other than a childminder F142... , and
(b) give the person a certificate of registration stating that he is so registered.

(3) Subsections (3) to (5) of section 64 apply in relation to a certificate of registration given in pursuance of subsection (1) or (2) of this section as they apply in relation to a certificate of registration given in pursuance of subsection (1) or (2) of that section.

Amendments (Textual)

F141. Words in s. 65 inserted (1.4.2014 for specified purposes, 1.9.2014 in so far as not already in force) by Children and Families Act 2014 (c. 6), s. 139. (6), Sch. 4 para. 28; S.I. 2014/889, arts. 3. (m), 7. (e)

F142. Words in s. 65. (2) omitted (1.1.2016) by virtue of Small Business, Enterprise and Employment Act 2015 (c. 26), s. 164. (1), Sch. 2 para. 14; S.I. 2015/1329, reg. 6. (b)

Commencement Information

I56. S. 65 in force at 1.9.2008 by S.I. 2008/2261, art. 2 (with Schs. 1, 2)

[F143. Voluntary registration of persons registered with childminder agencies

Amendments (Textual)

F143. S. 65. A and cross-heading inserted (1.4.2014 for specified purposes, 1.9.2014 in so far as not already in force) by Children and Families Act 2014 (c. 6), s. 139. (6), Sch. 4 para. 29; S.I. 2014/889, arts. 3. (m), 7. (e)

65. AProcedure for persons already registered with a childminder agency

(1) A person who is registered as an early years childminder with an early years childminder agency or as a later years childminder with a later years childminder agency may give notice to the agency that he or she wishes to be registered with the agency in respect of the provision in England of—

(a) later years childminding for a child who has attained the age of eight;
(b) early years childminding or later years childminding for a child who has not attained that age but in respect of which the person is not required to be registered under Chapter 2 or 3.

(2) If a person gives notice to an agency under subsection (1), the agency must—

(a) register the person in the register maintained by the agency as a childminder registered under this Chapter, and
(b) give the person a certificate of registration stating that he or she is so registered.

(3) A person who is registered as an early years provider (other than a childminder) with an early years childminder agency or as a later years provider (other than a childminder) with a later years childminder agency F144... may give notice to the agency that he or she wishes to be registered with the agency in respect of F144...—

(a) later years provision (other than later years childminding) for a child who has attained the age of eight;
(b) early years provision or later years provision (other than early years or later years

childminding) for a child who has not attained that age but in respect of which the person is not required to be registered under Chapter 2 or 3.
(4) If a person gives notice to an agency under subsection (3), the agency must—
(a) register the person in the register maintained by the agency as a provider of childcare (other than a childminder) registered under this Chapter F145..., and
(b) give the person a certificate of registration stating that he or she is so registered.
(5) A certificate of registration given to the applicant in pursuance of subsection (2) or (4) must contain prescribed information about prescribed matters.
(6) If there is a change of circumstances which requires the amendment of a certificate of registration, the agency must give the registered person an amended certificate.]
Amendments (Textual)
F144. Words in s. 65. A(3) omitted (1.1.2016) by virtue of Small Business, Enterprise and Employment Act 2015 (c. 26), s. 164. (1), Sch. 2 para. 15. (a); S.I. 2015/1329, reg. 6. (b)
F145. Words in s. 65. A(4) omitted (1.1.2016) by virtue of Small Business, Enterprise and Employment Act 2015 (c. 26), s. 164. (1), Sch. 2 para. 15. (b); S.I. 2015/1329, reg. 6. (b)

Regulation of persons registering voluntarily

66. Conditions on registration
(1) The Chief Inspector may impose such conditions as he thinks fit on the registration of a person [F146in Part B of the general childcare register].
(2) The power conferred by subsection (1) may be exercised at the time when the Chief Inspector registers a person in pursuance of section 64 or 65 or at any subsequent time.
(3) The Chief Inspector may at any time vary or remove any condition imposed under subsection (1).
(4) The power conferred by subsection (1) includes power to impose conditions for the purpose of giving effect to regulations under section 67.
(5) A person registered F147[in Part B of the general childcare register] commits an offence if, without reasonable excuse, he fails to comply with any condition imposed under subsection (1).
(6) A person guilty of an offence under subsection (5) is liable on summary conviction to a fine not exceeding level 5 on the standard scale.
Amendments (Textual)
F146. Words in s. 66. (1) substituted (1.4.2014 for specified purposes, 1.9.2014 in so far as not already in force) by Children and Families Act 2014 (c. 6), s. 139. (6), Sch. 4 para. 30; S.I. 2014/889, arts. 3. (m), 7. (e)
F147. Words in s. 66. (5) substituted (1.4.2014 for specified purposes, 1.9.2014 in so far as not already in force) by Children and Families Act 2014 (c. 6), s. 139. (6), Sch. 4 para. 30; S.I. 2014/889, arts. 3. (m), 7. (e)
Commencement Information
I57. S. 66 in force at 6.4.2007 by S.I. 2007/1019, art. 4
67. Regulations governing activities
(1) This section applies to persons providing early years provision or later years provision (or both) in respect of which they are registered under this Chapter.
(2) The Secretary of State may, after consulting the Chief Inspector and any other person he considers appropriate, make regulations governing the activities of persons to whom this section applies.
(3) The regulations may deal with the following matters (among others)—
   (a) the welfare of the children concerned;
   (b) the arrangements for safeguarding the children concerned;
   (c) suitability of persons to care for, or be in regular contact with, the children concerned;
   (d) qualifications and training;
   (e) the suitability of premises and equipment;

(f) the manner in which the childcare provision is organised;
(g) procedures for dealing with complaints;
(h) the keeping of records;
(i) the provision of information.

(4) The power to make regulations under this section may be exercised so as confer powers or impose duties on the Chief Inspector [F148, early years childminder agencies or later years childminder agencies] in the exercise of F149... functions under this Part.

(5) In particular, it may be so exercised so as to require the Chief Inspector [F150, early years childminder agencies or later years childminder agencies], in exercising F151... functions under this Part, to have regard to factors, standards and other matters prescribed by or referred to in the regulations.

(6) If the regulations require any person (other than the Chief Inspector) to have regard to or meet factors, standards and other matters prescribed by or referred to in the regulations, they may also provide for any allegation that the person has failed to do so to be taken into account—

(a) by the Chief Inspector in the exercise of his functions under this Part,

[F152. (aa)by early years childminder agencies or later years childminder agencies in the exercise of functions under this Part,] or

(b) in any proceedings under this Part.

Amendments (Textual)

F148. Words in s. 67. (4) inserted (1.4.2014 for specified purposes, 1.9.2014 in so far as not already in force) by Children and Families Act 2014 (c. 6), s. 139. (6), Sch. 4 para. 31. (2)(a); S.I. 2014/889, arts. 3. (m), 7. (e)

F149. Word in s. 67. (4) omitted (1.4.2014 for specified purposes, 1.9.2014 in so far as not already in force) by virtue of Children and Families Act 2014 (c. 6), s. 139. (6), Sch. 4 para. 31. (2)(b); S.I. 2014/889, arts. 3. (m), 7. (e)

F150. Words in s. 67. (5) inserted (1.4.2014 for specified purposes, 1.9.2014 in so far as not already in force) by Children and Families Act 2014 (c. 6), s. 139. (6), Sch. 4 para. 31. (3)(a); S.I. 2014/889, arts. 3. (m), 7. (e)

F151. Word in s. 67. (5) omitted (1.4.2014 for specified purposes, 1.9.2014 in so far as not already in force) by virtue of Children and Families Act 2014 (c. 6), s. 139. (6), Sch. 4 para. 31. (3)(b); S.I. 2014/889, arts. 3. (m), 7. (e)

F152. S. 67. (6)(aa) inserted (1.4.2014 for specified purposes, 1.9.2014 in so far as not already in force) by Children and Families Act 2014 (c. 6), s. 139. (6), Sch. 4 para. 31. (4); S.I. 2014/889, arts. 3. (m), 7. (e)

Commencement Information

I58. S. 67 in force at 20.12.2006 for specified purposes by S.I. 2006/3360, art. 2. (d)

I59. S. 67 in force at 6.4.2007 in so far as not already in force by S.I. 2007/1019, art. 4

Chapter 5. Common provisions

68. Cancellation of registration [F153in a childcare register: early years and later years providers]

(1) The Chief Inspector must cancel the registration of a person registered under Chapter 2, 3 or 4 [F154 in the early years register or the general childcare register] if it appears to him that the person has become disqualified from registration by regulations under section 75.

(2) The Chief Inspector may cancel the registration of a person registered under Chapter 2, 3 or 4 [F155in the early years register or the general childcare register] if it appears to him—

(a) that the prescribed requirements for registration which apply in relation to the person's registration under that Chapter have ceased, or will cease, to be satisfied,

(b) that the person has failed to comply with a condition imposed on his registration under that Chapter,

(c) that he has failed to comply with a requirement imposed on him by regulations under that Chapter,

(d) in the case of a person registered under Chapter 2 [F156in the early years register], that he has failed to comply with section 40. (2)(a), or

(e) in any case, that he has failed to pay a prescribed fee.

(3) The Chief Inspector may cancel the registration of a person registered [F157under Chapter 2 in the early years register as an early years childminder] if it appears to him that the person has not provided early years childminding for a period of more than three years during which he was registered.

(4) The Chief Inspector may cancel the registration of a person registered [F158under Chapter 3 in Part A of the general childcare register as a later years childminder] if it appears to him that the person has not provided later years childminding for a period of more than three years during which he was registered.

(5) The Chief Inspector may cancel the registration of a person registered [F159under Chapter 4 in Part B of the general childcare register as a childminder] if it appears to him that the person has provided neither early years childminding nor later years childminding for a period of more than three years during which he was registered.

(6) Where a requirement to make any changes or additions to any services, equipment or premises has been imposed on a person registered under Chapter 2, 3 or 4 [F160in the early years register or the general childcare register], his registration may not be cancelled on the ground of any defect or insufficiency in the services, equipment or premises if—

(a) the time set for complying with the requirements has not expired, and

(b) it is shown that the defect or insufficiency is due to the changes or additions not having been made.

Amendments (Textual)

F153. Words in s. 68 inserted (1.4.2014 for specified purposes, 1.9.2014 in so far as not already in force) by Children and Families Act 2014 (c. 6), s. 139. (6), Sch. 4 para. 33. (8); S.I. 2014/889, arts. 3. (m), 7. (e)

F154. Words in s. 68. (1) inserted (1.4.2014 for specified purposes, 1.9.2014 in so far as not already in force) by Children and Families Act 2014 (c. 6), s. 139. (6), Sch. 4 para. 33. (2); S.I. 2014/889, arts. 3. (m), 7. (e)

F155. Words in s. 68. (2) inserted (1.4.2014 for specified purposes, 1.9.2014 in so far as not already in force) by Children and Families Act 2014 (c. 6), s. 139. (6), Sch. 4 para. 33. (3)(a); S.I. 2014/889, arts. 3. (m), 7. (e)

F156. Words in s. 68. (2)(d) inserted (1.4.2014 for specified purposes, 1.9.2014 in so far as not already in force) by Children and Families Act 2014 (c. 6), s. 139. (6), Sch. 4 para. 33. (3)(b); S.I. 2014/889, arts. 3. (m), 7. (e)

F157. Words in s. 68. (3) substituted (1.4.2014 for specified purposes, 1.9.2014 in so far as not already in force) by Children and Families Act 2014 (c. 6), s. 139. (6), Sch. 4 para. 33. (4); S.I. 2014/889, arts. 3. (m), 7. (e)

F158. Words in s. 68. (4) substituted (1.4.2014 for specified purposes, 1.9.2014 in so far as not already in force) by Children and Families Act 2014 (c. 6), s. 139. (6), Sch. 4 para. 33. (5); S.I. 2014/889, arts. 3. (m), 7. (e)

F159. Words in s. 68. (5) substituted (1.4.2014 for specified purposes, 1.9.2014 in so far as not already in force) by Children and Families Act 2014 (c. 6), s. 139. (6), Sch. 4 para. 33. (6); S.I. 2014/889, arts. 3. (m), 7. (e)

F160. Words in s. 68. (6) inserted (1.4.2014 for specified purposes, 1.9.2014 in so far as not already in force) by Children and Families Act 2014 (c. 6), s. 139. (6), Sch. 4 para. 33. (7); S.I. 2014/889, arts. 3. (m), 7. (e)

Commencement Information

I60. S. 68 in force at 6.4.2007 by S.I. 2007/1019, art. 4

69. Suspension of registration [F161in a childcare register: early years and later years providers]

(1) Regulations may provide for the registration of a person registered under Chapter 2, 3 or 4 [F162in the early years register or the general childcare register] to be suspended for a prescribed period in prescribed circumstances.

[F163. (1. A)Regulations under subsection (1) may in particular provide that registration may be suspended generally or only in relation to particular premises.]

(2) Regulations under subsection (1) must include provision conferring on the registered person a right of appeal to the Tribunal against suspension.

(3) A person registered [F164under Chapter 2 in the early years register as an early years childminder] [F165—

(a) may not provide early years childminding at any time when his registration under that Chapter is suspended generally in accordance with regulations under this section;

(b) may not provide early years childminding on particular premises at any time when his registration under that Chapter is suspended in relation to those premises in accordance with regulations under this section.]

(4) A person registered [F166under Chapter 3 in Part A of the general childcare register as a later years childminder] [F167—

(a) may not provide later years childminding at any time when his registration under that Chapter is suspended generally in accordance with regulations under this section;

(b) may not provide later years childminding on particular premises at any time when his registration under that Chapter is suspended in relation to those premises in accordance with regulations under this section.]

(5) Subsection (3) or (4) does not apply in relation to early years childminding or (as the case may be) later years childminding which the person may provide without being registered under Chapter 2 or 3.

(6) A person registered [F168under Chapter 2 in the early years register as an early years provider (other than an early years childminder)] [F169—

(a) may not provide early years provision at any time when his registration under that Chapter is suspended generally in accordance with regulations under this section;

(b) may not provide early years provision on particular premises at any time when his registration under that Chapter is suspended in relation to those premises in accordance with regulations under this section.]

(7) A person registered [F170 under Chapter 3 in Part A of the general childcare register as a later years provider (other than a later years childminder)] [F171—

(a) may not provide later years provision, for a child who has not attained the age of 8, at any time when his registration under that Chapter is suspended generally in accordance with regulations under this section;

(b) may not provide later years provision, for a child who has not attained the age of 8, on particular premises at any time when his registration under that Chapter is suspended in relation to those premises in accordance with regulations under this section.]

(8) Subsection (6) or (7) does not apply in relation to early years provision or (as the case may be) later years provision which the person may provide without being registered under Chapter 2 or 3.

(9) A person commits an offence if, without reasonable excuse, he contravenes subsection (3), (4), (6) or (7).

(10) A person guilty of an offence under subsection (9) is liable on summary conviction to a fine not exceeding level 5 on the standard scale.

(11) In this Part, "the Tribunal" means the [F172. First-tier Tribunal].

Amendments (Textual)

F161. Words in s. 69 inserted (1.4.2014 for specified purposes, 1.9.2014 in so far as not already in force) by Children and Families Act 2014 (c. 6), s. 139. (6), Sch. 4 para. 34. (7); S.I. 2014/889, arts. 3. (m), 7. (e)

F162. Words in s. 69. (1) inserted (1.4.2014 for specified purposes, 1.9.2014 in so far as not already in force) by Children and Families Act 2014 (c. 6), s. 139. (6), Sch. 4 para. 34. (2); S.I. 2014/889, arts. 3. (m), 7. (e)

F163. S. 69. (1. A) inserted (15.6.2015) by Small Business, Enterprise and Employment Act 2015 (c. 26), s. 164. (1), Sch. 2 para. 16. (a); S.I. 2015/1329, reg. 4

F164. Words in s. 69. (3) substituted (1.4.2014 for specified purposes, 1.9.2014 in so far as not already in force) by Children and Families Act 2014 (c. 6), s. 139. (6), Sch. 4 para. 34. (3); S.I. 2014/889, arts. 3. (m), 7. (e)

F165. Words in s. 69. (3) substituted (1.1.2016) by Small Business, Enterprise and Employment Act 2015 (c. 26), s. 164. (1), Sch. 2 para. 16. (b); S.I. 2015/1329, reg. 6. (b)

F166. Words in s. 69. (4) substituted (1.4.2014 for specified purposes, 1.9.2014 in so far as not already in force) by Children and Families Act 2014 (c. 6), s. 139. (6), Sch. 4 para. 34. (4); S.I. 2014/889, arts. 3. (m), 7. (e)

F167. Words in s. 69. (4) substituted (1.1.2016) by Small Business, Enterprise and Employment Act 2015 (c. 26), s. 164. (1), Sch. 2 para. 16. (c); S.I. 2015/1329, reg. 6. (b)

F168. Words in s. 69. (6) substituted (1.4.2014 for specified purposes, 1.9.2014 in so far as not already in force) by Children and Families Act 2014 (c. 6), s. 139. (6), Sch. 4 para. 34. (5); S.I. 2014/889, arts. 3. (m), 7. (e)

F169. Words in s. 69. (6) substituted (1.1.2016) by Small Business, Enterprise and Employment Act 2015 (c. 26), s. 164. (1), Sch. 2 para. 16. (d); S.I. 2015/1329, reg. 6. (b)

F170. Words in s. 69. (7) substituted (1.4.2014 for specified purposes, 1.9.2014 in so far as not already in force) by Children and Families Act 2014 (c. 6), s. 139. (6), Sch. 4 para. 34. (6); S.I. 2014/889, arts. 3. (m), 7. (e)

F171. Words in s. 69. (7) substituted (1.1.2016) by Small Business, Enterprise and Employment Act 2015 (c. 26), s. 164. (1), Sch. 2 para. 16. (e); S.I. 2015/1329, reg. 6. (b)

F172. Words in s. 69. (11) substituted (3.11.2008) by The Transfer of Tribunal Functions Order 2008 (S.I. 2008/2833), art. 1. (1), Sch. 3 para. 221

Commencement Information

I61. S. 69 in force at 20.12.2006 for specified purposes by S.I. 2006/3360, art. 2. (d)

I62. S. 69 in force at 6.4.2007 in so far as not already in force by S.I. 2007/1019, art. 4

[F17369. ACancellation, termination and suspension of registration with a childminder agency

(1) Regulations may make provision about the cancellation, termination and suspension of the registration of an early years provider or a later years provider with an early years childminder agency or a later years childminder agency for the purposes of Chapter 2, 3 or 4, in particular—

(a) about the termination by an early years provider or a later years provider of his or her registration;

(b) for the creation of offences relating to things done while a registration is suspended;

(c) about the resolution of disputes between an early years provider or a later years provider and an early years childminder agency or a later years childminder agency.

(2) Regulations by virtue of subsection (1) which make provision about the suspension of the registration of an early years provider or a later years provider with a childminder agency must include provision conferring on the registered provider a right of appeal to the Tribunal against suspension.

(3) Regulations made by virtue of subsection (1)(b) may only create offences which are—

(a) triable only summarily, and

(b) punishable only with a fine not exceeding the level specified in the regulations, which may not exceed level 5 on the standard scale.]

Amendments (Textual)

F173. S. 69. A inserted (1.4.2014 for specified purposes, 1.9.2014 in so far as not already in force) by Children and Families Act 2014 (c. 6), s. 139. (6), Sch. 4 para. 35; S.I. 2014/889, arts. 3. (m), 7. (e)

[F17469. BCancellation of registration: childminder agencies

(1) The Chief Inspector must cancel the registration of a person registered under Chapter 2. A or 3. A as an early years childminder agency or a later years childminder agency if it appears to the Chief Inspector that the person has become disqualified from registration by regulations under section 76. A.

(2) The Chief Inspector may cancel the registration of a person registered under Chapter 2. A or 3. A as an early years childminder agency or a later years childminder agency if it appears to the Chief Inspector—

(a) that the prescribed requirements for registration which apply in relation to the person's registration under that Chapter have ceased, or will cease, to be satisfied,

(b) that the person has failed to comply with a condition imposed on the registration under that Chapter,

(c) that the person has failed to comply with a requirement imposed by regulations under that Chapter,

(d) that the person has failed to comply with a requirement imposed by this Chapter, or by regulations under this Chapter, or

(e) that the person has failed to pay a prescribed fee.

(3) Where a requirement to make any changes or additions to any services has been imposed on a person registered under Chapter 2. A or 3. A as an early years childminder agency or a later years childminder agency, the person's registration may not be cancelled on the ground of any defect or insufficiency in the services, if—

(a) the time set for complying with the requirements has not expired, and

(b) it is shown that the defect or insufficiency is due to the changes or additions not having been made.

(4) Regulations may make provision about the effect of the cancellation under this section of the registration under Chapter 2. A or 3. A of an early years childminder agency or a later years childminder agency on an early years provider or a later years provider registered with the agency for the purposes of Chapter 2, 3 or 4.

Amendments (Textual)

F174. Ss. 69. B, 69. C inserted (1.4.2014 for specified purposes, 1.9.2014 in so far as not already in force) by Children and Families Act 2014 (c. 6), s. 139. (6), Sch. 4 para. 36; S.I. 2014/889, arts. 3. (m), 7. (e)

69. CSuspension of registration: childminder agencies

(1) Regulations may provide for the registration of a person registered under Chapter 2. A or 3. A as an early years childminder agency or a later years childminder agency to be suspended for a prescribed period in prescribed circumstances.

(2) Regulations under subsection (1) must include provision conferring on the registered person a right of appeal to the Tribunal against suspension.

(3) Regulations under subsection (1) may make provision about the effect of the suspension of the registration of an early years childminder agency or a later years childminder agency on an early years provider or a later years provider registered with the agency for the purposes of Chapter 2, 3 or 4.

(4) A person registered under Chapter 2. A as an early years childminder agency may not, at any time when the person's registration under that Chapter is suspended in accordance with regulations under this section—

(a) exercise any functions of an early years childminder agency, or

(b) represent that the person may exercise such functions.

(5) A person registered under Chapter 3. A as a later years childminder agency may not, at any time when the person's registration under that Chapter is suspended in accordance with regulations under this section—

(a) exercise any functions of a later years childminder agency, or

(b) represent that the person may exercise such functions.

(6) A person commits an offence if, without reasonable excuse, the person contravenes subsection (4) or (5).

(7) A person guilty of an offence under subsection (6) is liable on summary conviction to a fine not exceeding level 5 on the standard scale.]

Amendments (Textual)

F174. Ss. 69. B, 69. C inserted (1.4.2014 for specified purposes, 1.9.2014 in so far as not already in force) by Children and Families Act 2014 (c. 6), s. 139. (6), Sch. 4 para. 36; S.I. 2014/889, arts. 3. (m), 7. (e)

70. Voluntary removal from [F175a childcare register: early years and later years providers]

(1) A person registered under [F176. Chapter 2, 3 or 4] may give notice to the Chief Inspector that he wishes to be removed from the early years register or (as the case may be) from Part A or B of the general childcare register.

(2) If a person gives notice under subsection (1) the Chief Inspector must remove him from the early years register or (as the case may be) from the relevant Part of the general childcare register.

(3) The Chief Inspector must not act under subsection (2) if—

(a) the Chief Inspector has sent the person a notice (in pursuance of section 73. (2)) of his intention to cancel his registration, and

(b) the Chief Inspector has not decided that he no longer intends to take that step.

(4) The Chief Inspector must not act under subsection (2) if—

(a) the Chief Inspector has sent the person a notice (in pursuance of section 73. (7)) of his decision to cancel his registration, and

(b) the time within which an appeal under section 74 may be brought has not expired or, if such an appeal has been brought, it has not been determined.

(5) Subsections (3) and (4) do not apply if the person is seeking removal from Part B of the general childcare register.

Amendments (Textual)

F175. Words in s. 70 substituted (1.4.2014 for specified purposes, 1.9.2014 in so far as not already in force) by Children and Families Act 2014 (c. 6), s. 139. (6), Sch. 4 para. 37. (3); S.I. 2014/889, arts. 3. (m), 7. (e)

F176. Words in s. 70. (1) substituted (1.4.2014 for specified purposes, 1.9.2014 in so far as not already in force) by Children and Families Act 2014 (c. 6), s. 139. (6), Sch. 4 para. 37. (2); S.I. 2014/889, arts. 3. (m), 7. (e)

Commencement Information

I63. S. 70 in force at 6.4.2007 by S.I. 2007/1019, art. 4

[F17770. AVoluntary removal from a childcare register: childminder agencies

(1) A person registered under Chapter 2. A or 3. A as an early years childminder agency or a later years childminder agency may give notice to the Chief Inspector of a wish to be removed from the early years register or (as the case may be) from Part A of the general childcare register.

(2) If a person gives notice under subsection (1) the Chief Inspector must remove the person from the early years register or (as the case may be) from Part A of the general childcare register.

(3) The Chief Inspector must not act under subsection (2) if—

(a) the Chief Inspector has sent the person a notice (in pursuance of section 73. (2)) of the Chief Inspector's intention to cancel the person's registration, and

(b) the Chief Inspector has not decided that he or she no longer intends to take that step.

(4) The Chief Inspector must not act under subsection (2) if—

(a) the Chief Inspector has sent the person a notice (in pursuance of section 73. (7)) of the Chief Inspector's decision to cancel the person's registration, and

(b) the time within which an appeal under section 74 may be brought has not expired or, if such an appeal has been brought, it has not been determined.]

Amendments (Textual)

F177. S. 70. A inserted (1.4.2014 for specified purposes, 1.9.2014 in so far as not already in force) by Children and Families Act 2014 (c. 6), s. 139. (6), Sch. 4 para. 38; S.I. 2014/889, arts. 3. (m), 7. (e)

71. Termination of voluntary registration [F178in Part B of the general childcare register] on expiry of prescribed period

Regulations may make provision requiring the Chief Inspector to remove a registered person from Part B of the general childcare register on the expiry of a prescribed period of time from the date of his registration.

Amendments (Textual)

F178. Words in s. 71 inserted (1.4.2014 for specified purposes, 1.9.2014 in so far as not already in force) by Children and Families Act 2014 (c. 6), s. 139. (6), Sch. 4 para. 39; S.I. 2014/889, arts. 3. (m), 7. (e)

Commencement Information

I64. S. 71 in force at 20.12.2006 by S.I. 2006/3360, art. 2. (e)

Cancellation etc. in an emergency

72. Protection of children in an emergency

(1) In relation to a person registered under Chapter 2, 3 or 4 [F179in the early years register or the general childcare register], the Chief Inspector may apply to [F180the family court] for an order—

(a) cancelling the person's registration;

(b) varying or removing a condition to which his registration is subject;

(c) imposing a new condition on his registration.

(2) If it appears to [F181the court] that a child for whom early years provision or later years provision is being or may be provided by that person is suffering or is likely to suffer significant harm, [F181the court] may make the order.

(3) An application under subsection (1) may be made without notice.

(4) An order under subsection (2)—

(a) must be made in writing, and

(b) has effect from the time when it is made.

(5) If an order is made under subsection (2), the Chief Inspector must serve on the registered person as soon as is reasonably practicable after the making of the order—

(a) a copy of the order,

(b) a copy of any written statement in support of the application for the order, and

(c) notice of any right of appeal conferred by section 74.

(6) The documents mentioned in subsection (5) may be served on the registered person by—

(a) delivering them to him, or

(b) sending them by post.

(7) For the purposes of this section, "harm" has the same meaning as in the Children Act 1989 (c. 41) and the question of whether harm is significant is to be determined in accordance with section 31. (10) of that Act.

Amendments (Textual)

F179. Words in s. 72. (1) inserted (1.4.2014 for specified purposes, 1.9.2014 in so far as not already in force) by Children and Families Act 2014 (c. 6), s. 139. (6), Sch. 4 para. 40; S.I. 2014/889, arts. 3. (m), 7. (e)

F180. Words in s. 72. (1) substituted (22.4.2014) by Crime and Courts Act 2013 (c. 22), s. 61. (3), Sch. 11 para. 203. (a); S.I. 2014/954, art. 2. (e) (with art. 3) (with transitional provisions and savings in S.I. 2014/956, arts. 3-11)

F181. Words in s. 72. (2) substituted (22.4.2014) by Crime and Courts Act 2013 (c. 22), s. 61. (3), Sch. 11 para. 203. (b); S.I. 2014/954, art. 2. (e) (with art. 3) (with transitional provisions and savings in S.I. 2014/956, arts. 3-11)

Commencement Information

I65. S. 72 in force at 6.4.2007 by S.I. 2007/1019, art. 4

Registration – procedural safeguards

73. Procedure for taking certain steps

(1) This section applies if the Chief Inspector proposes to take any of the following steps under this Part—

(a) refuse an application for registration;

(b) impose a new condition on a person's registration;

(c) vary or remove any condition imposed on a person's registration;

(d) refuse to grant an application for the variation or removal of any such condition;

(e) cancel a person's registration.

(2) The Chief Inspector must give to the applicant or (as the case may be) the registered person notice of his intention to take the step in question.

(3) The notice must—

(a) give the Chief Inspector's reasons for proposing to take the step, and

(b) inform the person concerned of [F182the person's] rights under this section.

(4) The Chief Inspector may not take the step until the end of the period of 14 days beginning with the day on which he gives notice under subsection (2) unless the applicant or (as the case may be) the registered person notifies the Chief Inspector that [F183the applicant or registered person] does not wish to object to the step being taken.

(5) If the recipient of a notice under subsection (2) ("the recipient") gives notice to the Chief Inspector that [F184the recipient] wishes to object to the step being taken, the Chief Inspector must give [F185the recipient] an opportunity to object before deciding whether to take the step.

(6) An objection made in pursuance of subsection (5) may be made orally or in writing and in either case may be made by the recipient or [F186the recipient's] representative.

(7) If the Chief Inspector decides to take the step, he must give the recipient notice of his decision (whether or not the recipient informed the Chief Inspector that [F187the recipient] wished to object to the step being taken).

(8) The taking of a step mentioned in paragraph (b), (c) or (e) of subsection (1) does not have effect until—

(a) the expiry of the time within which an appeal may be brought under section 74, or

(b) if such an appeal is brought, the time when the appeal is determined (and the taking of the step is confirmed).

(9) Subsection (8) does not prevent such a step having effect before the expiry of the time within which an appeal may be brought if the person concerned notifies the Chief Inspector that [F188the person] does not intend to appeal.

(10) If the Chief Inspector gives notice to an applicant for registration under Chapter 2 or 3 that he intends to refuse [F189the] application, the application may not be withdrawn without the consent of the Chief Inspector.

(11) In this section and in section 74, "a new condition" means a condition imposed otherwise than at the time of the person's registration.

Amendments (Textual)

F182. Words in s. 73. (3)(b) substituted (1.4.2014 for specified purposes, 1.9.2014 in so far as not already in force) by Children and Families Act 2014 (c. 6), s. 139. (6), Sch. 4 para. 41. (2); S.I. 2014/889, arts. 3. (m), 7. (e)

F183. Words in s. 73. (4) substituted (1.4.2014 for specified purposes, 1.9.2014 in so far as not already in force) by Children and Families Act 2014 (c. 6), s. 139. (6), Sch. 4 para. 41. (3); S.I. 2014/889, arts. 3. (m), 7. (e)

F184. Words in s. 73. (5) substituted (1.4.2014 for specified purposes, 1.9.2014 in so far as not already in force) by Children and Families Act 2014 (c. 6), s. 139. (6), Sch. 4 para. 41. (4)(a); S.I. 2014/889, arts. 3. (m), 7. (e)

F185. Words in s. 73. (5) substituted (1.4.2014 for specified purposes, 1.9.2014 in so far as not already in force) by Children and Families Act 2014 (c. 6), s. 139. (6), Sch. 4 para. 41. (4)(b); S.I. 2014/889, arts. 3. (m), 7. (e)

F186. Words in s. 73. (6) substituted (1.4.2014 for specified purposes, 1.9.2014 in so far as not already in force) by Children and Families Act 2014 (c. 6), s. 139. (6), Sch. 4 para. 41. (5); S.I. 2014/889, arts. 3. (m), 7. (e)

F187. Words in s. 73. (7) substituted (1.4.2014 for specified purposes, 1.9.2014 in so far as not already in force) by Children and Families Act 2014 (c. 6), s. 139. (6), Sch. 4 para. 41. (6); S.I. 2014/889, arts. 3. (m), 7. (e)

F188. Words in s. 73. (9) substituted (1.4.2014 for specified purposes, 1.9.2014 in so far as not already in force) by Children and Families Act 2014 (c. 6), s. 139. (6), Sch. 4 para. 41. (7); S.I. 2014/889, arts. 3. (m), 7. (e)

F189. Word in s. 73. (10) substituted (1.4.2014 for specified purposes, 1.9.2014 in so far as not already in force) by Children and Families Act 2014 (c. 6), s. 139. (6), Sch. 4 para. 41. (8); S.I. 2014/889, arts. 3. (m), 7. (e)

Commencement Information

I66. S. 73 in force at 6.4.2007 by S.I. 2007/1019, art. 4

74. Appeals [F190relating to registration in a childcare register]

(1) An applicant for registration or (as the case may be) a registered person may appeal to the Tribunal against the taking of any of the following steps by the Chief Inspector under this Part—

(a) the refusal of [F191the] application for registration;

(b) the imposition of a new condition on [F192the person's] registration;

(c) the variation or removal of any condition imposed on [F193the person's] registration;

(d) the refusal of an application to vary or remove any such condition;

(e) the cancellation of [F194the person's] registration.

(2) An applicant for registration or (as the case may be) a registered person may also appeal to the Tribunal against any other determination made by the Chief Inspector under this Part which is of a prescribed description.

(3) A person against whom an order is made under section 72. (2) may appeal to the Tribunal against the making of the order.

(4) On an appeal the Tribunal must either—

(a) confirm the taking of the step, the making of the other determination or the making of the order (as the case may be), or

(b) direct that it shall not have, or shall cease to have, effect.

(5) Unless the Tribunal has confirmed the taking of a step mentioned in subsection (1)(a) or (e) or the making of an order under section 72. (2) cancelling a person's registration, the Tribunal may also do either or both of the following—

(a) impose conditions on the registration of the person concerned;

(b) vary or remove any condition previously imposed on [F195the] registration.

Amendments (Textual)

F190. Words in s. 74 inserted (1.4.2014 for specified purposes, 1.9.2014 in so far as not already in force) by Children and Families Act 2014 (c. 6), s. 139. (6), Sch. 4 para. 42. (4); S.I. 2014/889, arts. 3. (m), 7. (e)

F191. Word in s. 74. (1)(a) substituted (1.4.2014 for specified purposes, 1.9.2014 in so far as not already in force) by Children and Families Act 2014 (c. 6), s. 139. (6), Sch. 4 para. 42. (2)(a); S.I. 2014/889, arts. 3. (m), 7. (e)

F192. Words in s. 74. (1)(b) substituted (1.4.2014 for specified purposes, 1.9.2014 in so far as not already in force) by Children and Families Act 2014 (c. 6), s. 139. (6), Sch. 4 para. 42. (2)(b); S.I. 2014/889, arts. 3. (m), 7. (e)

F193. Words in s. 74. (1)(c) substituted (1.4.2014 for specified purposes, 1.9.2014 in so far as not already in force) by Children and Families Act 2014 (c. 6), s. 139. (6), Sch. 4 para. 42. (2)(c); S.I. 2014/889, arts. 3. (m), 7. (e)

F194. Words in s. 74. (1)(e) substituted (1.4.2014 for specified purposes, 1.9.2014 in so far as not already in force) by Children and Families Act 2014 (c. 6), s. 139. (6), Sch. 4 para. 42. (2)(d); S.I. 2014/889, arts. 3. (m), 7. (e)

F195. Word in s. 74. (5)(b) substituted (1.4.2014 for specified purposes, 1.9.2014 in so far as not already in force) by Children and Families Act 2014 (c. 6), s. 139. (6), Sch. 4 para. 42. (3); S.I. 2014/889, arts. 3. (m), 7. (e)

Commencement Information

I67. S. 74 in force at 20.12.2006 for specified purposes by S.I. 2006/3360, art. 2. (d)

I68. S. 74 in force at 6.4.2007 in so far as not already in force by S.I. 2007/1019, art. 4

Disqualification from registration [F196: early years and later years providers]

Amendments (Textual)
F196. Words in Pt. 3 Ch. 5. (crossheading)(disqualification)(from)(registration) inserted (1.4.2014 for specified purposes, 1.9.2014 in so far as not already in force) by Children and Families Act 2014 (c. 6), s. 139. (6), Sch. 4 para. 43; S.I. 2014/889, arts. 3. (m), 7. (e)

75. Disqualification from registration[F197: early years and later years providers]

(1) In this section, "registration" means registration under Chapters 2, 3 and 4.
(2) Regulations may provide for a person to be disqualified from registration.
(3) The regulations may, in particular, provide for a person to be disqualified from registration if—
   (a) he is included in the list kept under section 1 of the Protection of Children Act 1999 (c. 14);
   (b) he is subject to a direction under section 142 of the Education Act 2002 (c. 32) on the grounds that he is unsuitable to work with children or on grounds relating to his health;
   [F198. (ba)he is barred from regulated activity relating to children (within the meaning of section 3. (2) of the Safeguarding Vulnerable Groups Act 2006);]
   (c) an order of a prescribed kind has been made at any time with respect to him;
   (d) an order of a prescribed kind has been made at any time with respect to a child who has been in his care;
   (e) a requirement of a prescribed kind has been imposed at any time with respect to such a child, under or by virtue of any enactment;
   (f) he has at any time been refused registration under Chapter 2, 3 or 4 of this Part of this Act or under Part 10 or Part 10. A of the Children Act 1989 (c. 41) [F199or under Part 2 of the Children and Families (Wales) Measure 2010] or any prescribed enactment, or had any such registration cancelled;
   (g) he has been convicted of an offence of a prescribed kind or has been discharged absolutely or conditionally for such an offence;
   (h) he has been given a caution in respect of an offence of a prescribed kind;
   (i) he has at any time been disqualified from fostering a child privately (within the meaning of the Children Act 1989 (c. 41));
   (j) a prohibition has been imposed on him at any time under section 69 of the Children Act 1989, section 10 of the Foster Children (Scotland) Act 1984 (c. 56) or any prescribed enactment;
   (k) his rights and powers with respect to a child have at any time been vested in a prescribed authority under a prescribed enactment.
(4) Regulations may provide for a person to be disqualified from registration if—
   (a) he lives in the same household as another person who is disqualified from registration, or
   (b) he lives in a household in which any such person is employed.
(5) Regulations under subsection (2) or (4) may provide for a person not to be disqualified from registration (and in particular may provide for a person not to be disqualified from registration for the purposes of section 76) by reason of any fact which would otherwise cause him to be disqualified if—
   (a) he has disclosed the fact to the Chief Inspector, and
   (b) the Chief Inspector has consented in writing to the person's not being disqualified from registration and has not withdrawn his consent.
(6) In this section—
F200...
"enactment" means any enactment having effect at any time in any part of the United Kingdom.
(7) A conviction in respect of which a probation order was made before 1st October 1992 (which would not otherwise be treated as a conviction) is to be treated as a conviction for the purposes of this section.

Amendments (Textual)
F197. Words in s. 75 inserted (1.4.2014 for specified purposes, 1.9.2014 in so far as not already in force) by Children and Families Act 2014 (c. 6), s. 139. (6), Sch. 4 para. 44; S.I. 2014/889, arts. 3. (m), 7. (e)

F198. S. 75. (3)(ba) inserted (19.5.2008) by Safeguarding Vulnerable Groups Act 2006 (c. 47), s. 65, Sch. 9 para. 10. (1) (with ss. 51, 57. (3), 60. (4), 64. (5)); S.I. 2008/1320, art. 2. (d)
F199. Words in s. 75. (3)(f) inserted (W.) (1.4.2011) by Children and Families (Wales) Measure 2010 (nawm 1), s. 75. (3), Sch. 1 para. 23; S.I. 2010/2582, art. 2, Sch. 1 (with Schs. 2 3)
F200. Words in s. 75. (6) omitted (8.4.2013) by virtue of Legal Aid, Sentencing and Punishment of Offenders Act 2012 (c. 10), s. 151. (1), Sch. 24 para. 27 (with s. 135. (4)); S.I. 2013/453, art. 4. (f)
Commencement Information
I69. S. 75 in force at 20.12.2006 by S.I. 2006/3360, art. 2. (e)
76. Consequences of disqualification [F201: early years and later years providers]
(1) This section applies to—
    (a) early years provision in respect of which the provider is required by section 33. (1) or 34. (1) [F202or (1. A)] to be registered,
    (b) early years provision in respect of which, but for section 34. (2), the provider would be required to be registered,
    (c) later years provision in respect of which the provider is required by section 52. (1) or 53. (1) [F203or (1. A)] to be registered, and
    (d) later years provision in respect of which, but for section 53. (2), the provider would be required to be registered.
(2) A person who is disqualified from registration by regulations under section 75 must not—
    (a) provide early years or later years provision to which this section applies, or
    (b) be directly concerned in the management of early years or later years provision to which this section applies.
(3) No person may employ, in connection with the provision of early years or later years provision to which this section applies, a person who is disqualified from registration by regulations under section 75.
[F204. (3. A)An early years childminder agency must not register for the purposes of Chapter 2 a person who is disqualified from registration by regulations under section 75.
(3. B)A later years childminder agency must not register for the purposes of Chapter 3 a person who is disqualified from registration by regulations under section 75.
(3. C)An early years childminder agency or a later years childminder agency must not register for the purposes of Chapter 4 a person who is disqualified from registration by regulations under section 75.]
(4) A person who contravenes subsection (2) [F205, (3), (3. A), (3. B) or (3. C)] commits an offence.
(5) A person who contravenes subsection (2) is not guilty of an offence under subsection (4) if—
    (a) he is disqualified from registration by virtue only of regulations under section 75. (4), and
    (b) he proves that he did not know, and had no reasonable grounds for believing, that he was living—
(i) in the same household as a person who was disqualified from registration, or
(ii) in a household in which such a person was employed.
(6) A person [F206. ("A")] who contravenes subsection (3) is not guilty of an offence under subsection (4) if [F207. A] proves that [F207. A] did not know, and had no reasonable grounds for believing, that the person whom [F207. A] was employing was disqualified from registration.
[F208. (6. A)A person ("A") who contravenes subsection (3. A), (3. B) or (3. C) is not guilty of an offence under subsection (4) if A proves that A did not know, and had no reasonable grounds for believing, that the person registered by A was disqualified from registration.]
(7) A person guilty of an offence under subsection (4) is liable on summary conviction to imprisonment for a term not exceeding 51 weeks, or to a fine not exceeding level 5 on the standard scale, or to both.
(8) In relation to an offence committed before the commencement of section 281. (5) of the Criminal Justice Act 2003 (c. 44) (alteration of penalties for summary offences), the reference in subsection (7) to 51 weeks is to be read as a reference to 6 months.

Amendments (Textual)
F201. Words in s. 76 inserted (1.4.2014 for specified purposes, 1.9.2014 in so far as not already in force) by Children and Families Act 2014 (c. 6), s. 139. (6), Sch. 4 para. 45. (7); S.I. 2014/889, arts. 3. (m), 7. (e)
F202. Words in s. 76. (1)(a) inserted (1.4.2014 for specified purposes, 1.9.2014 in so far as not already in force) by Children and Families Act 2014 (c. 6), s. 139. (6), Sch. 4 para. 45. (2)(a); S.I. 2014/889, arts. 3. (m), 7. (e)
F203. Words in s. 76. (1)(c) inserted (1.4.2014 for specified purposes, 1.9.2014 in so far as not already in force) by Children and Families Act 2014 (c. 6), s. 139. (6), Sch. 4 para. 45. (2)(b); S.I. 2014/889, arts. 3. (m), 7. (e)
F204. S. 76. (3. A)-(3. C) inserted (1.4.2014 for specified purposes, 1.9.2014 in so far as not already in force) by Children and Families Act 2014 (c. 6), s. 139. (6), Sch. 4 para. 45. (3); S.I. 2014/889, arts. 3. (m), 7. (e)
F205. Words in s. 76. (4) substituted (1.4.2014 for specified purposes, 1.9.2014 in so far as not already in force) by Children and Families Act 2014 (c. 6), s. 139. (6), Sch. 4 para. 45. (4); S.I. 2014/889, arts. 3. (m), 7. (e)
F206. Words in s. 76. (6) inserted (1.4.2014 for specified purposes, 1.9.2014 in so far as not already in force) by Children and Families Act 2014 (c. 6), s. 139. (6), Sch. 4 para. 45. (5)(a); S.I. 2014/889, arts. 3. (m), 7. (e)
F207. Word in s. 76. (6) substituted (1.4.2014 for specified purposes, 1.9.2014 in so far as not already in force) by Children and Families Act 2014 (c. 6), s. 139. (6), Sch. 4 para. 45. (5)(b); S.I. 2014/889, arts. 3. (m), 7. (e)
F208. S. 76. (6. A) inserted (1.4.2014 for specified purposes, 1.9.2014 in so far as not already in force) by Children and Families Act 2014 (c. 6), s. 139. (6), Sch. 4 para. 45. (6); S.I. 2014/889, arts. 3. (m), 7. (e)

[F209. Disqualification from registration: childminder agencies

Amendments (Textual)
F209. Ss. 76. A, 76. B and cross-heading inserted (1.4.2014 for specified purposes, 1.9.2014 in so far as not already in force) by Children and Families Act 2014 (c. 6), s. 139. (6), Sch. 4 para. 46; S.I. 2014/889, arts. 3. (m), 7. (e)
76. ADisqualification from registration: childminder agencies
(1) In this section, " registration " means registration under Chapter 2. A or 3. A.
(2) Regulations may provide for a person to be disqualified from registration.
(3) Regulations under subsection (2) may provide for a person not to be disqualified from registration (and in particular may provide for a person not to be disqualified from registration for the purposes of section 76. B) by reason of any fact which would otherwise cause the person to be disqualified if—
    (a) the person has disclosed the fact to the Chief Inspector, and
    (b) the Chief Inspector has consented in writing to the person's not being disqualified from registration and has not withdrawn the consent.
76. BConsequences of disqualification: childminder agencies
(1) A person who is disqualified from registration by regulations under section 76. A must not—
    (a) exercise any functions of an early years childminder agency or a later years childminder agency,
    (b) represent that the person can exercise such functions,
    (c) be a director, manager or other officer of, or partner in, an early years childminder agency or a later years childminder agency, be a member of the governing body of such an agency, or otherwise be directly concerned in the management of such an agency, or
    (d) work for such an agency in any capacity which involves entering premises on which early years provision or later years provision is being provided.

(2) No early years childminder agency or later years childminder agency may employ a person who is disqualified from registration by regulations under section 76. A in any capacity which involves—
   (a) being directly concerned in the management of an early years childminder agency or a later years childminder agency, or
   (b) entering premises on which early years provision or later years provision is being provided.
(3) A person who contravenes subsection (1) or (2) commits an offence.
(4) A person ("P") who contravenes subsection (2) is not guilty of an offence under subsection (3) if P proves that P did not know, and had no reasonable grounds for believing, that the person whom P was employing was disqualified from registration.
(5) A person guilty of an offence under subsection (3) is liable on summary conviction to imprisonment for a term not exceeding 51 weeks, or to a fine not exceeding level 5 on the standard scale, or to both.
(6) In relation to an offence committed before the commencement of section 281. (5) of the Criminal Justice Act 2003 (c. 44) (alteration of penalties for summary offences), the reference in subsection (5) to 51 weeks is to be read as a reference to 6 months.]

Rights of entry

77[F210. Chief Inspector's powers of entry: early years provision and later years provision]
(1) F211... the Chief Inspector may at any reasonable time enter any premises in England if he has reasonable cause to believe that early years provision or later years provision is being provided on the premises in breach of section 33. (1), 34. (1) [F212or (1. A)], 52. (1) or 53. (1) [F213or (1. A)].
(2) F214... the Chief Inspector may at any reasonable time enter any premises in England on which early years provision or later years provision in respect of which a person is registered under this Part is being provided—
   (a) for the purpose of conducting an inspection under section 49 [F215, 51. D(2), 60 or 61. E(2)], or
   (b) for the purpose of determining whether any conditions or requirements imposed by or under this Part are being complied with.
(3) [F216. An authorisation given by the Chief Inspector under paragraph 9. (1) of Schedule 12 to the Education and Inspections Act 2006 in relation to his functions] under subsection (1) or (2)—
   (a) may be given for a particular occasion or period;
   (b) may be given subject to conditions.
(4) A person entering premises under this section may (subject to any conditions imposed under subsection (3)(b))—
   (a) inspect the premises;
   (b) inspect, and take copies of—
(i) any records kept by the person providing the childcare, and
(ii) any other documents containing information relating to that provision;
   (c) seize and remove any document or other material or thing found there which he has reasonable grounds to believe may be evidence of a failure to comply with any condition or requirement imposed by or under this Part;
   (d) take measurements and photographs or make recordings;
   (e) inspect any children being cared for there, and the arrangements made for their welfare;
   (f) interview in private the childcare provider;
   (g) interview in private any person caring for children, or living or working, on the premises who consents to be interviewed.
(5) A person entering premises under this section may (subject to any conditions imposed under subsection (3)(b)) require any person to afford him such facilities and assistance with respect to matters within the person's control as are necessary to enable him to exercise his powers under this section.

(6) Section 58 of the Education Act 2005 (c. 18) (inspection of computer records for the purposes of Part 1 of that Act) applies for the purposes of this section as it applies for the purposes of Part 1 of that Act.

F217. (7). . . . .

(8) A person commits an offence if he intentionally obstructs a person exercising any power under this section.

(9) A person guilty of an offence under subsection (8) is liable on summary conviction to a fine not exceeding level 4 on the standard scale.

(10) In this section, "documents" and "records" each include information recorded in any form.

Amendments (Textual)

F210. Words in s. 77 substituted (1.4.2014 for specified purposes, 1.9.2014 in so far as not already in force) by Children and Families Act 2014 (c. 6), s. 139. (6), Sch. 4 para. 47. (4); S.I. 2014/889, arts. 3. (m), 7. (e)

F211. Words in s. 77. (1) repealed (1.4.2007) by Education and Inspections Act 2006 (c. 40), s. 188. (3), Sch. 14 para. 113. (2), Sch. 18 Pt. 5; S.I. 2007/935, art. 5. (gg)(ii)

F212. Words in s. 77. (1) inserted (1.4.2014 for specified purposes, 1.9.2014 in so far as not already in force) by Children and Families Act 2014 (c. 6), s. 139. (6), Sch. 4 para. 47. (2)(a); S.I. 2014/889, arts. 3. (m), 7. (e)

F213. Words in s. 77. (1) inserted (1.4.2014 for specified purposes, 1.9.2014 in so far as not already in force) by Children and Families Act 2014 (c. 6), s. 139. (6), Sch. 4 para. 47. (2)(b); S.I. 2014/889, arts. 3. (m), 7. (e)

F214. Words in s. 77. (2) repealed (1.4.2007) by Education and Inspections Act 2006 (c. 40), s. 188. (3), Sch. 14 para. 113. (2), Sch. 18 Pt. 5; S.I. 2007/935, art. 5. (gg)(ii)

F215. Words in s. 77. (2)(a) substituted (1.4.2014 for specified purposes, 1.9.2014 in so far as not already in force) by Children and Families Act 2014 (c. 6), s. 139. (6), Sch. 4 para. 47. (3); S.I. 2014/889, arts. 3. (m), 7. (e)

F216. Word in s. 77. (3) substituted (1.4.2007) by Education and Inspections Act 2006 (c. 40), s. 188. (3), Sch. 14 para. 113. (3); S.I. 2007/935, art. 5. (gg)

F217. S. 77. (7) repealed (1.4.2007) by Education and Inspections Act 2006 (c. 40), s. 188. (3), Sch. 14 para. 113. (4), Sch. 18 Pt. 5; S.I. 2007/935, art. 5. (gg)(ii)

Commencement Information

I70. S. 77 in force at 6.4.2007 by S.I. 2007/1019, art. 4

78[F218. Powers of entry under section 77: requirement for consent]

(1) This section applies where a person ("the authorised person") proposes to enter domestic premises in pursuance of—

(a) provision made by virtue of section 42. (1) and (4) in a learning and development order specifying assessment arrangements in relation to early years provision, or

(b) a power of entry conferred by section 77. (2).

(2) If the authorised person has reasonable cause to believe—

(a) that the premises are not the home of the person providing the early years or later years provision, or

(b) that the premises are the home of a child for whom the early years or later years provision is provided,

the authorised person may not enter the premises without the consent of an adult who is an occupier of the premises.

(3) Subsection (2) does not prevent the imposition under section 38, 58 or 66 of a condition requiring a person registered under Chapter 2, 3 or 4 to secure that the occupier of any premises on which the registered person provides early years provision or later years provision gives any consent required by that subsection.

(4) In this section—

"a learning and development order" means an order under section 39. (1)(a);

"occupier" does not include the person providing the early years or later years rovision.

Amendments (Textual)

F218. S. 78 substituted (1.4.2014 for specified purposes, 1.9.2014 in so far as not already in force) by Children and Families Act 2014 (c. 6), s. 139. (6), Sch. 4 para. 48; S.I. 2014/889, arts. 3. (m), 7. (e)

Commencement Information

I71. S. 78 in force at 6.4.2007 by S.I. 2007/1019, art. 4

[F219 78. A Chief Inspector's powers of entry: childminder agencies

(1) The Chief Inspector may at any reasonable time enter any premises in England if the Chief Inspector has reasonable cause to believe that a person on the premises is falsely representing—

    (a) that the person is an early years childminder agency, or

    (b) that the person is a later years childminder agency.

(2) The Chief Inspector may at any reasonable time enter any premises in England which is registered in—

    (a) the early years register as premises of an early years childminder agency, or

    (b) Part A of the general childcare register as premises of a later years childminder agency,

for any of the purposes in subsection (3).

(3) Those purposes are—

    (a) conducting an inspection under section 51. D(1) or 61. E(1);

    (b) determining whether any conditions or requirements imposed by or under this Part are being complied with.

(4) An authorisation given by the Chief Inspector under paragraph 9. (1) of Schedule 12 to the Education and Inspections Act 2006 in relation to the functions under subsection (1) or (2)—

    (a) may be given for a particular occasion or period;

    (b) may be given subject to conditions.

(5) A person entering premises under this section may (subject to any conditions imposed under subsection (4)(b))—

    (a) inspect the premises;

    (b) inspect, and take copies of—

(i) any records kept concerning early years providers or later years providers, and

(ii) any other documents containing information relating to such providers;

    (c) seize and remove any document or other material or thing found there which the person has reasonable grounds to believe may be evidence of a failure to comply with any condition or requirement imposed by or under this Part;

    (d) take measurements and photographs or make recordings;

    (e) interview in private any person present on the premises who works there.

(6) A person entering premises under this section may (subject to any conditions imposed under subsection (4)(b)) require any person to afford such facilities and assistance with respect to matters within the person's control as are necessary to enable the powers under this section to be exercised.

(7) Section 58 of the Education Act 2005 (inspection of computer records for the purposes of Part 1 of that Act) applies for the purposes of this section as it applies for the purposes of Part 1 of that Act.

(8) It is an offence intentionally to obstruct a person exercising any power under this section.

(9) A person guilty of an offence under subsection (8) is liable on summary conviction to a fine not exceeding level 4 on the standard scale.

(10) In this section, "documents" and "records" each include information recorded in any form.

Amendments (Textual)

F219. Ss. 78. A, 78. B inserted (1.4.2014 for specified purposes) by Children and Families Act 2014 (c. 6), s. 139. (6), Sch. 4 para. 49; S.I. 2014/889, art. 3. (m)

F22078. BPowers of entry under section 78. A: requirement for consent

(1) This section applies where a person (" the authorised person ") proposes to enter domestic premises in pursuance of a power of entry conferred by section 78. A(2).

(2) If the authorised person has reasonable cause to believe that the premises are the home of a person who—

    (a) is not employed by the early years childminder agency or (as the case may be) the later years childminder agency, or

(b) is not a director, manager or other officer of, or partner in, the agency, a member of its governing body or otherwise directly concerned in the management of the agency,

the authorised person may not enter the premises without the consent of an adult who is an occupier of the premises and who falls within paragraph (a) or (b).]

Amendments (Textual)

F219. Ss. 78. A, 78. B inserted (1.4.2014 for specified purposes) by Children and Families Act 2014 (c. 6), s. 139. (6), Sch. 4 para. 49; S.I. 2014/889, art. 3. (m)

F220. Ss. 78. A, 78. B inserted (1.4.2014 for specified purposes, 1.9.2014 in so far as not already in force) by Children and Families Act 2014 (c. 6), s. 139. (6), Sch. 4 para. 49; S.I. 2014/889, arts. 3. (m), 7. (e)

79. Power of constable to assist in exercise of powers of entry

(1) [F221. The Chief Inspector] may apply to a court for a warrant under this section.

(2) If it appears to the court that the [F222 Chief Inspector]—

(a) has attempted to exercise a power conferred on him by section 77 [F223or 78. A] but has been prevented from doing so, or

(b) is likely to be prevented from exercising any such power,

the court may issue a warrant authorising any constable to assist [F224the Chief Inspector] in the exercise of the power, using reasonable force if necessary.

(3) A warrant issued under this section must be addressed to, and executed by, a constable.

F225. (4). . . . .

(5) In this section, "court" means the High Court [F226or the family court].

Amendments (Textual)

F221. Words in s. 79. (1) substituted (1.4.2007) by Education and Inspections Act 2006 (c. 40), s. 188. (3), Sch. 14 para. 114. (2); S.I. 2007/935, art. 5. (gg)

F222. Words in s. 79. (2) substituted (1.4.2007) by Education and Inspections Act 2006 (c. 40), s. 188. (3), Sch. 14 para. 114. (3)(a); S.I. 2007/935, art. 5. (gg)

F223. Words in s. 79. (2)(a) inserted (1.4.2014 for specified purposes, 1.9.2014 in so far as not already in force) by Children and Families Act 2014 (c. 6), s. 139. (6), Sch. 4 para. 50; S.I. 2014/889, arts. 3. (m), 7. (e)

F224. Words in s. 79. (2) substituted (1.4.2007) by Education and Inspections Act 2006 (c. 40), s. 188. (3), Sch. 14 para. 114. (3)(b); S.I. 2007/935, art. 5. (gg)

F225. S. 79. (4) omitted (22.4.2014) by virtue of Crime and Courts Act 2013 (c. 22), s. 61. (3), Sch. 11 para. 204. (a); S.I. 2014/954, art. 2. (e) (with art. 3) (with transitional provisions and savings in S.I. 2014/956, arts. 3-11)

F226. Words in s. 79. (5) substituted (22.4.2014) by Crime and Courts Act 2013 (c. 22), s. 61. (3), Sch. 11 para. 204. (b); S.I. 2014/954, art. 2. (e) (with art. 3) (with transitional provisions and savings in S.I. 2014/956, arts. 3-11)

Commencement Information

I72. S. 79 in force at 6.4.2007 by S.I. 2007/1019, art. 4

Reports and information

Prospective

F22780. Combined reports

. . . .

Amendments (Textual)

F227. S. 80 repealed (1.4.2007) by Education and Inspections Act 2006 (c. 40), s. 188. (3), Sch. 14 para. 115, Sch. 18 Pt. 5; S.I. 2007/935, art. 5. (gg)(ii)

Prospective

F22881. Information to be included in annual reports

. . . .

Amendments (Textual)
F228. S. 81 repealed (1.4.2007) by Education and Inspections Act 2006 (c. 40), s. 188. (3), Sch. 14 para. 116, Sch. 18 Pt. 5; S.I. 2007/935, art. 5. (gg)(ii)

82. Supply of information to Chief Inspector

[F229. (1)] The Chief Inspector may at any time require any person registered under this Part to provide him with any information connected with the person's activities as an early years provider or later years provider [F230, or (as the case may be) as an early years childminder agency or later years childminder agency,] which the Chief Inspector considers it necessary to have for the purposes of his functions under this Part.

[F231. (2)The Chief Inspector's power under subsection (1) includes a power to require an early years childminder agency or a later years childminder agency to provide the Chief Inspector with information about an early years provider or a later years provider registered with the agency for the purposes of Chapter 2, 3 or 4.]

Amendments (Textual)
F229. S. 82. (1): s. 82 renumbered as s. 82. (1) (1.4.2014 for specified purposes, 1.9.2014 in so far as not already in force) by Children and Families Act 2014 (c. 6), s. 139. (6), Sch. 4 para. 51. (2); S.I. 2014/889, arts. 3. (m), 7. (e)
F230. Words in s. 82. (1) inserted (1.4.2014 for specified purposes, 1.9.2014 in so far as not already in force) by Children and Families Act 2014 (c. 6), s. 139. (6), Sch. 4 para. 51. (3); S.I. 2014/889, arts. 3. (m), 7. (e)
F231. S. 82. (2) inserted (1.4.2014 for specified purposes, 1.9.2014 in so far as not already in force) by Children and Families Act 2014 (c. 6), s. 139. (6), Sch. 4 para. 51. (4); S.I. 2014/889, arts. 3. (m), 7. (e)

Commencement Information
I73. S. 82 in force at 6.4.2007 by S.I. 2007/1019, art. 4

83. Supply of information to [F232the Secretary of State,] HMRC and local authorities [F233by the Chief Inspector]

(1) The Chief Inspector must provide prescribed information to [F234the Secretary of State,] Her Majesty's Revenue and Customs, and the relevant local authority, if he takes any of the following steps under this Part—

(a) grants a person's application for registration;

(b) gives notice of his intention to cancel a person's registration;

(c) cancels a person's registration;

(d) suspends a person's registration;

(e) removes a person from the register at that person's request.

(2) The Chief Inspector must also provide prescribed information to [F234the Secretary of State,] Her Majesty's Revenue and Customs, and the relevant local authority, if an order is made under section 72. (2).

(3) The information which may be prescribed for the purposes of this section is—

(a) in the case of information to be provided to Her Majesty's Revenue and Customs, information which Her Majesty's Revenue and Customs may require for the purposes of their functions in relation to tax credits;

[F235. (aa)in the case of information to be provided to the Secretary of State, information which the Secretary of State may require for the purposes of the Secretary of State's functions in relation to universal credit;]

(b) in the case of information to be provided to the relevant local authority, information which would assist the local authority in the discharge of their functions under section 12.

(4) In this section, "the relevant local authority" means the English local authority for the area in which [F236—

(a)]the person provides (or, as the case may be, has provided) the early years provision or later years provision in respect of which he is (or was) registered.[F237;

(b) registered premises of the early years childminder agency or later years childminder agency are (or, as the case may be, were) located.]

Amendments (Textual)
F232. Words in s. 83 heading inserted (29.4.2013) by The Universal Credit (Consequential, Supplementary, Incidental and Miscellaneous Provisions) Regulations 2013 (S.I. 2013/630), regs. 1. (2), 19. (3)(a)
F233. Words in s. 83 inserted (1.4.2014 for specified purposes, 1.9.2014 in so far as not already in force) by Children and Families Act 2014 (c. 6), s. 139. (6), Sch. 4 para. 52. (3); S.I. 2014/889, arts. 3. (m), 7. (e)
F234. Words in s. 83. (1)(2) inserted (29.4.2013) by The Universal Credit (Consequential, Supplementary, Incidental and Miscellaneous Provisions) Regulations 2013 (S.I. 2013/630), regs. 1. (2), 19. (3)(b)
F235. S. 83. (3)(aa) inserted (29.4.2013) by The Universal Credit (Consequential, Supplementary, Incidental and Miscellaneous Provisions) Regulations 2013 (S.I. 2013/630), regs. 1. (2), 19. (3)(c)
F236. Word in s. 83. (4) inserted (1.4.2014 for specified purposes, 1.9.2014 in so far as not already in force) by Children and Families Act 2014 (c. 6), s. 139. (6), Sch. 4 para. 52. (2)(a); S.I. 2014/889, arts. 3. (m), 7. (e)
F237. S. 83. (4)(b) inserted (1.4.2014 for specified purposes, 1.9.2014 in so far as not already in force) by Children and Families Act 2014 (c. 6), s. 139. (6), Sch. 4 para. 52. (2)(b); S.I. 2014/889, arts. 3. (m), 7. (e)
Commencement Information
I74. S. 83 in force at 20.12.2006 for specified purposes by S.I. 2006/3360, art. 2. (d)
I75. S. 83 in force at 6.4.2007 in so far as not already in force by S.I. 2007/1019, art. 4
[F23883. A Supply of information to the Secretary of State, HMRC and local authorities by childminder agencies
(1) An early years childminder agency or a later years childminder agency must provide prescribed information to the Secretary of State, Her Majesty's Revenue and Customs, and each relevant local authority, if it—
　(a) grants a person's application for registration for the purposes of Chapter 2, 3 or 4;
　(b) takes any other steps under this Part of a prescribed description.
(2) The information which may be prescribed for the purposes of this section is—
　(a) in the case of information to be provided to the Secretary of State, information which the Secretary of State may require for the purposes of the Secretary of State's functions in relation to universal credit under Part 1 of the Welfare Reform Act 2012;
　(b) in the case of information to be provided to Her Majesty's Revenue and Customs, information which Her Majesty's Revenue and Customs may require [F239for the purposes of—
(i) their functions in relation to tax credits, or
(ii) their functions under the Childcare Payments Act 2014;]
　(c) in the case of information to be provided to a relevant local authority, information which would assist the local authority in the discharge of their functions under section 12.
(3) In this section, " relevant local authority " means an English local authority for an area in which a person who is (or, as the case may be, was) registered with the early years childminder agency or later years childminder agency for the purposes of Chapter 2 or 3 provides (or has provided) early years provision or later years provision in respect of which he or she is (or was) registered.]
Amendments (Textual)
F238. S. 83. A inserted (1.4.2014 for specified purposes, 1.9.2014 in so far as not already in force) by Children and Families Act 2014 (c. 6), s. 139. (6), Sch. 4 para. 53; S.I. 2014/889, arts. 3. (m), 7. (e)
F239. Words in s. 83. A(2)(b) substituted (20.7.2016) by Childcare Payments Act 2014 (c. 28), ss. 29, 75. (2); S.I. 2016/763, reg. 2. (1)
84. Disclosure of information for certain purposes [F240: the Chief Inspector]
(1) The Chief Inspector may arrange for prescribed information held by him in relation to persons registered under this Part to be made available for the purpose of—41
　(a) assisting parents or prospective parents in choosing an early years or later years provider, or

(b) protecting children from harm or neglect.

(2) The information may be made available in such manner and to such persons as the Chief Inspector considers appropriate.

(3) Regulations may require the Chief Inspector to provide prescribed information held by him in relation to persons registered under this Part to prescribed persons for either of the purposes mentioned in subsection (1).

Amendments (Textual)

F240. Words in s. 84 inserted (1.4.2014 for specified purposes, 1.9.2014 in so far as not already in force) by Children and Families Act 2014 (c. 6), s. 139. (6), Sch. 4 para. 54; S.I. 2014/889, arts. 3. (m), 7. (e)

Commencement Information

I76. S. 84 in force at 20.12.2006 for specified purposes by S.I. 2006/3360, art. 2. (d)

I77. S. 84 in force at 6.4.2007 in so far as not already in force by S.I. 2007/1019, art. 4

[F24184. ADisclosure of information for certain purposes: childminder agencies

(1) An early years childminder agency or a later years childminder agency may arrange for prescribed information held by the agency in relation to persons registered with the agency under this Part to be made available for the purpose of—

(a) assisting parents or prospective parents in choosing an early years provider or later years provider, or

(b) protecting children from harm or neglect.

(2) The information may be made available in such manner and to such persons as the agency considers appropriate.

(3) Regulations may require an early years childminder agency or a later years childminder agency to provide prescribed information held by the agency in relation to persons registered with the agency under this Part to prescribed persons for either of the purposes mentioned in subsection (1).]

Amendments (Textual)

F241. S. 84. A inserted (1.4.2014 for specified purposes, 1.9.2014 in so far as not already in force) by Children and Families Act 2014 (c. 6), s. 139. (6), Sch. 4 para. 55; S.I. 2014/889, arts. 3. (m), 7. (e)

Offences and criminal proceedings

85. Offence of making false or misleading statement

(1) A person commits an offence if, in an application for registration under any of Chapters 2 to 4, [F242 the person] knowingly makes a statement which is false or misleading in a material particular.

(2) A person guilty of an offence under subsection (1) is liable on summary conviction to a fine not exceeding level 5 on the standard scale.

Amendments (Textual)

F242. Words in s. 85. (1) substituted (1.4.2014 for specified purposes, 1.9.2014 in so far as not already in force) by Children and Families Act 2014 (c. 6), s. 139. (6), Sch. 4 para. 56; S.I. 2014/889, arts. 3. (m), 7. (e)

Commencement Information

I78. S. 85 in force at 6.4.2007 by S.I. 2007/1019, art. 4

[F24385. AOffence of providing provision other than on approved premises

The Secretary of State may by regulations provide—

(a) that a person who without reasonable excuse fails to comply with a prescribed requirement falling within section 35. (5)(b), 36. (5)(b), 54. (5)(b) or 55. (5)(b) (premises) is guilty of an offence, and

(b) that a person guilty of the offence is liable on summary conviction to a fine.]

Amendments (Textual)

F243. S. 85. A inserted (15.6.2015) by Small Business, Enterprise and Employment Act 2015 (c. 26), s. 164. (1), Sch. 2 para. 17; S.I. 2015/1329, reg. 4

86. Time limit for proceedings

(1) Proceedings for an offence under this Part or regulations made under it may be brought within a period of six months from the date on which evidence sufficient in the opinion of the prosecutor to warrant the proceedings comes to his knowledge.

(2) No such proceedings may be brought by virtue of subsection (1) more than three years after the commission of the offence.

Commencement Information

I79. S. 86 in force at 6.4.2007 by S.I. 2007/1019, art. 4

87. Offences by bodies corporate [F244and partnerships]

(1) [F245. Subsection (2)] applies where any offence under this Part is committed by a body corporate.

(2) If the offence is proved to have been committed with the consent or connivance of, or to be attributable to any neglect on the part of, any director, manager or other similar officer of the body corporate, or any person who was purporting to act in any such capacity, he (as well as the body corporate) is guilty of the offence and liable to be proceeded against and punished accordingly.

[F246. (3)Subsection (4) applies where any offence under this Part is committed by a partnership.

(4) If the offence is proved to have been committed with the consent or connivance of, or to be attributable to any neglect on the part of, any partner, that partner (as well as the partnership) is guilty of the offence and liable to be proceeded against and punished accordingly.]

Amendments (Textual)

F244. Words in s. 87 inserted (1.4.2014 for specified purposes, 1.9.2014 in so far as not already in force) by Children and Families Act 2014 (c. 6), s. 139. (6), Sch. 4 para. 57. (4); S.I. 2014/889, arts. 3. (m), 7. (e)

F245. Words in s. 87. (1) substituted (1.4.2014 for specified purposes, 1.9.2014 in so far as not already in force) by Children and Families Act 2014 (c. 6), s. 139. (6), Sch. 4 para. 57. (2); S.I. 2014/889, arts. 3. (m), 7. (e)

F246. S. 87. (3)(4) inserted (1.4.2014 for specified purposes, 1.9.2014 in so far as not already in force) by Children and Families Act 2014 (c. 6), s. 139. (6), Sch. 4 para. 57. (3); S.I. 2014/889, arts. 3. (m), 7. (e)

Commencement Information

I80. S. 87 in force at 6.4.2007 by S.I. 2007/1019, art. 4

88. Unincorporated associations

(1) Proceedings for an offence under this Part which is alleged to have been committed by an unincorporated association must be brought in the name of the association (and not in the name of any of its members).

(2) For the purpose of any such proceedings, rules of court relating to the service of documents are to have effect as if the association were a body corporate.

(3) In proceedings for an offence under this Part brought against an unincorporated association, section 33 of the Criminal Justice Act 1925 (c. 86) and Schedule 3 to the Magistrates' Courts Act 1980 (c. 43) (procedure) apply as they do in relation to a body corporate.

(4) A fine imposed on an unincorporated association on its conviction of an offence under this Part is to be paid out of the funds of the association.

(5) If an offence under this Part by an unincorporated association is shown—

　(a) to have been committed with the consent or connivance of an officer of the association or a member of its governing body, or

　(b) to be attributable to any neglect on the part of such an officer or member,

the officer or member as well as the association is guilty of the offence and liable to be proceeded against and punished accordingly.

Commencement Information

I81. S. 88 in force at 6.4.2007 by S.I. 2007/1019, art. 4

Miscellaneous

89. Fees

(1) Regulations may require persons registered under any of Chapters 2 to 4 [F247in the early years register or the general childcare register] to pay to the Chief Inspector at or by prescribed times fees of the prescribed amounts in respect of the discharge by the Chief Inspector of his functions under this Part.

(2) Regulations under subsection (1) may prescribe circumstances in which—

(a) the amount of a fee payable under the regulations may be varied in accordance with the regulations;

(b) a fee payable under the regulations may be waived.

Amendments (Textual)

F247. Words in s. 89. (1) inserted (1.4.2014 for specified purposes, 1.9.2014 in so far as not already in force) by Children and Families Act 2014 (c. 6), s. 139. (6), Sch. 4 para. 58; S.I. 2014/889, arts. 3. (m), 7. (e)

Commencement Information

I82. S. 89 in force at 20.12.2006 by S.I. 2006/3360, art. 2. (e)

90. Cases where consent to disclosure withheld

(1) This section applies where the Chief Inspector—

(a) is determining, for the purpose of deciding whether to grant an application for registration under [F248any of Chapters 2 to 4], whether the prescribed requirements for registration are satisfied and are likely to be continued to be satisfied, or

(b) is determining, for the purpose of deciding whether to cancel the registration of any person under section 68. (2)(a) [F249or 69. B(2)(a)], whether the prescribed requirements for registration have ceased, or will cease, to be satisfied.

(2) The Chief Inspector may, if regulations so provide and he thinks it appropriate to do so, treat the prescribed requirements for registration as not being satisfied or (as the case may be) as having ceased to be satisfied if for the purpose of his determination—

(a) the Chief Inspector has requested a person ("A") to consent to the disclosure by another person ("B") to the Chief Inspector of information which—

(i) relates to A,

(ii) is held by B, and

(iii) is of a prescribed description, and

(b) A does not give F250... consent or withdraws F250... consent after giving it.

Amendments (Textual)

F248. Words in s. 90. (1)(a) substituted (1.4.2014 for specified purposes, 1.9.2014 in so far as not already in force) by Children and Families Act 2014 (c. 6), s. 139. (6), Sch. 4 para. 59. (2)(a); S.I. 2014/889, arts. 3. (m), 7. (e)

F249. Words in s. 90. (1)(b) inserted (1.4.2014 for specified purposes, 1.9.2014 in so far as not already in force) by Children and Families Act 2014 (c. 6), s. 139. (6), Sch. 4 para. 59. (2)(b); S.I. 2014/889, arts. 3. (m), 7. (e)

F250. Words in s. 90. (2)(b) omitted (1.4.2014 for specified purposes, 1.9.2014 in so far as not already in force) by virtue of Children and Families Act 2014 (c. 6), s. 139. (6), Sch. 4 para. 59. (3); S.I. 2014/889, arts. 3. (m), 7. (e)

Commencement Information

I83. S. 90 in force at 20.12.2006 for specified purposes by S.I. 2006/3360, art. 2. (d)

I84. S. 90 in force at 6.4.2007 in so far as not already in force by S.I. 2007/1019, art. 4

91. Co-operation between authorities

(1) If it appears to the Chief Inspector that any English local authority could, by taking any specified action, help in the exercise of any of his functions under this Part, he may request the help of the authority, specifying the action in question.

(2) An authority whose help is requested must comply with the request if it is compatible with

their own statutory and other duties and does not unduly prejudice the discharge of any of their functions.

Commencement Information

I85. S. 91 in force at 6.4.2007 by S.I. 2007/1019, art. 4

92. Combined certificates of registration

(1) This section applies if the Chief Inspector is required by virtue of this Part to issue more than one certificate of registration to a person.

(2) If the Chief Inspector considers it appropriate, he may combine any two or more of those certificates in a single certificate (a combined certificate).

(3) A combined certificate of registration must contain prescribed information about prescribed matters.

(4) If there is a change of circumstances which requires the amendment of a combined certificate of registration, the Chief Inspector must give the registered person an amended combined certificate.

(5) If the Chief Inspector is satisfied that a combined certificate of registration has been lost or destroyed, the Chief Inspector must give the registered person a copy, on payment by that person of any prescribed fee.

Commencement Information

I86. S. 92 in force at 20.12.2006 for specified purposes by S.I. 2006/3360, art. 2. (d)

I87. S. 92 in force at 1.9.2008 in so far as not already in force by S.I. 2008/2261, art. 2 (with Schs. 1, 2)

93. Notices

(1) This section applies in relation to notices required or authorised to be given to any person by any of the following—

   (a) section 57. (1) and (2);

   [F251. (aa)section 57. A(2) and (4);

   (ab) section 61. C(1);]

   (b) section 65. (1) and (2);

   [F252. (ba)section 65. A(1) and (3);]

   (c) section 70. (1);

   (d) section 73. (2), (4), (5), (7) and (9).

(2) The notice may be given to the person in question—

   (a) by delivering it to [F253the person],

   (b) by sending it by post, or

   (c) subject to subsection (3), by transmitting it electronically.

(3) If the notice is transmitted electronically, it is to be treated as given only if the requirements of subsection (4) or (5) are met.

(4) If the person required or authorised to give the notice is the Chief Inspector—

   (a) the person to whom the notice is required or authorised to be given must have indicated to the Chief Inspector [F254a] willingness to receive notices transmitted by electronic means and provided an address suitable for that purpose, and

   (b) the notice must be sent to the address provided F255....

(5) If the person required or authorised to give the notice is not the Chief Inspector, the notice must be transmitted in such manner as the Chief Inspector may require.

(6) An indication given for the purposes of subsection (4) may be given generally for the purposes of notices required or authorised to be given by the Chief Inspector under this Part or may be limited to notices of a particular description.

(7) A requirement imposed by the Chief Inspector under subsection (5) must be published in such manner as the Chief Inspector thinks appropriate for the purpose of bringing it to the attention of persons who are likely to be affected by it.

(8) In relation to the taking of a step mentioned in subsection (1)(b) or (c) of section 73, notification authorised to be given to the Chief Inspector under subsection (4) or (9) of that section may be given orally to a person authorised by the Chief Inspector to receive such notification (as

well as by any of the methods mentioned in subsection (2)).
Amendments (Textual)
F251. S. 93. (1)(aa)(ab) inserted (1.4.2014 for specified purposes, 1.9.2014 in so far as not already in force) by Children and Families Act 2014 (c. 6), s. 139. (6), Sch. 4 para. 60. (2)(a); S.I. 2014/889, arts. 3. (m), 7. (e)
F252. S. 93. (1)(ba) inserted (1.4.2014 for specified purposes, 1.9.2014 in so far as not already in force) by Children and Families Act 2014 (c. 6), s. 139. (6), Sch. 4 para. 60. (2)(a); S.I. 2014/889, arts. 3. (m), 7. (e)
F253. Words in s. 93. (2)(a) substituted (1.4.2014 for specified purposes, 1.9.2014 in so far as not already in force) by Children and Families Act 2014 (c. 6), s. 139. (6), Sch. 4 para. 60. (3); S.I. 2014/889, arts. 3. (m), 7. (e)
F254. Word in s. 93. (4)(a) substituted (1.4.2014 for specified purposes, 1.9.2014 in so far as not already in force) by Children and Families Act 2014 (c. 6), s. 139. (6), Sch. 4 para. 60. (4)(a); S.I. 2014/889, arts. 3. (m), 7. (e)
F255. Words in s. 93. (4)(b) omitted (1.4.2014 for specified purposes, 1.9.2014 in so far as not already in force) by virtue of Children and Families Act 2014 (c. 6), s. 139. (6), Sch. 4 para. 60. (4)(b); S.I. 2014/889, arts. 3. (m), 7. (e)
Commencement Information
I88. S. 93 in force at 6.4.2007 by S.I. 2007/1019, art. 4
F25694. Power to amend Part 3: applications in respect of multiple premises
. . . .
Amendments (Textual)
F256. S. 94 omitted (1.1.2016) by virtue of Small Business, Enterprise and Employment Act 2015 (c. 26), s. 164. (1), Sch. 2 para. 18; S.I. 2015/1329, reg. 6. (b)
95. Certain institutions not to be regarded as schools
(1) Section 4 of the Education Act 1996 (c. 56) (schools: general) is amended as follows.
(2) In subsection (1) after "In this Act" insert " (subject to subsection (1. A)) ".
(3) After subsection (1) insert—
"(1. A)An institution which—
    (a) provides only early years provision (as defined by section 96. (2) of the Childcare Act 2006), and
    (b) is not a maintained nursery school,
is not a school."
Commencement Information
I89. S. 95 in force at 1.9.2008 by S.I. 2008/2261, art. 2 (with Schs. 1, 2)

Interpretation

96. Meaning of early years and later years provision etc.
(1) This section applies for the purposes of this Part.
(2) "Early years provision" means the provision of childcare for a young child.
(3) "Early years provider" means a person who provides early years provision.
(4) Subject to subsection (5), "early years childminding" means early years provision F257... for reward[F258, where at least half of the provision is on domestic premises] (and "early years childminder" is to be read accordingly).
(5) Early years provision [F259which would otherwise fall within subsection (4)] is not early years childminding if at any time the number of persons providing the early years provision F260... or assisting with the provision exceeds three.
(6) "Later years provision", in relation to a child, means the provision of childcare at any time during the period—
    (a) beginning with the 1st September next following the date on which he attains the age of five, and

(b) ending with such day as may be prescribed.

(7) "Later years provider" means a person who provides later years provision.

(8) Subject to subsection (9), "later years childminding" means later years provision F261... for reward[F262, where at least half of the provision is on domestic premises] (and "later years childminder" is to be read accordingly).

(9) Later years provision [F263which would otherwise fall within subsection (8)] is not later years childminding if at any time the number of persons providing the later years provision F264... or assisting with the provision exceeds three.

Amendments (Textual)

F257. Words in s. 96. (4) omitted (1.1.2016) by virtue of Small Business, Enterprise and Employment Act 2015 (c. 26), ss. 76. (2)(a), 164. (1); S.I. 2015/1329, reg. 6. (a)

F258. Words in s. 96. (4) inserted (1.1.2016) by Small Business, Enterprise and Employment Act 2015 (c. 26), ss. 76. (2)(b), 164. (1); S.I. 2015/1329, reg. 6. (a)

F259. Words in s. 96. (5) substituted (1.1.2016) by Small Business, Enterprise and Employment Act 2015 (c. 26), ss. 76. (3)(a), 164. (1); S.I. 2015/1329, reg. 6. (a)

F260. Words in s. 96. (5) omitted (1.1.2016) by virtue of Small Business, Enterprise and Employment Act 2015 (c. 26), ss. 76. (3)(b), 164. (1); S.I. 2015/1329, reg. 6. (a)

F261. Words in s. 96. (8) omitted (1.1.2016) by virtue of Small Business, Enterprise and Employment Act 2015 (c. 26), ss. 76. (4)(a), 164. (1); S.I. 2015/1329, reg. 6. (a)

F262. Words in s. 96. (8) inserted (1.1.2016) by Small Business, Enterprise and Employment Act 2015 (c. 26), ss. 76. (4)(b), 164. (1); S.I. 2015/1329, reg. 6. (a)

F263. Words in s. 96. (9) substituted (1.1.2016) by Small Business, Enterprise and Employment Act 2015 (c. 26), ss. 76. (5)(a), 164. (1); S.I. 2015/1329, reg. 6. (a)

F264. Words in s. 96. (9) omitted (1.1.2016) by virtue of Small Business, Enterprise and Employment Act 2015 (c. 26), ss. 76. (5)(b), 164. (1); S.I. 2015/1329, reg. 6. (a)

Commencement Information

I90. S. 96 in force at 20.12.2006 for specified purposes by S.I. 2006/3360, art. 2. (d)

I91. S. 96 in force at 6.4.2007 in so far as not already in force by S.I. 2007/1019, art. 4

97. Employees not to be regarded as providing childcare

(1) This section applies for the purposes of this Part.

(2) Where an individual ("the employee") is employed to care for a child by a person who provides early years provision or later years provision for the child, the employee is not to be regarded as providing early years provision or (as the case may be) later years provision by virtue of anything done by him in the course of that employment.

Commencement Information

I92. S. 97 in force at 6.4.2007 by S.I. 2007/1019, art. 4

98. Interpretation of Part 3.

(1) In this Part—

"the Chief Inspector" means [F265. Her Majesty's Chief Inspector of Education, Children's Services and Skills];

"childcare" has the meaning given by section 18;

[F266" childminder agency " means—
  - an early years childminder agency;
  - a later years childminder agency;]

"domestic premises" means premises which are used wholly or mainly as a private dwelling;

[F267" early years childminder agency " means a person registered in the early years register as an early years childminder agency;]

"early years provision" has the meaning given by section 96. (2);

"early years provider" has the meaning given by section 96. (3);

"early years childminding" and "early years childminder" have the meanings given by section 96. (4);

[F268" later years childminder agency " means a person registered in Part A of the general childcare register as a later years childminder agency;]

"later years provision" has the meaning given by section 96. (6);
"later years provider" has the meaning given by section 96. (7);
"later years childminding" and "later years childminder" have the meanings given by section 96. (8);
"premises" includes any area and any vehicle;
F269...
"proprietor", in relation to a school, has the same meaning as in the Education Act 1996 (c. 56);
F269...
"the Tribunal" has the meaning given by section 69. (11);
"young child" has the meaning given by section 19.
[F270. (1. A)A person is registered for the purposes of this Part if that person is registered—
   (a) in the early years register,
   (b) in the general childcare register, or
   (c) with an early years childminder agency or a later years childminder agency.]
(2) For the purposes of section 7 of the Interpretation Act 1978 (c. 30) (references to service by post), a notice or order which may by virtue of any provision of this Part be sent by post to an applicant for registration or to a registered person is to be treated as properly addressed if it is addressed to him at the address notified by him to the Chief Inspector as the address to which correspondence to him should be sent.

Amendments (Textual)
F265. Words in s. 98. (1) substituted (1.4.2007) by Education and Inspections Act 2006 (c. 40), s. 188. (3), Sch. 14 para. 117; S.I. 2007/935, art. 5. (gg)
F266. Words in s. 98. (1) inserted (1.4.2014 for specified purposes, 1.9.2014 in so far as not already in force) by Children and Families Act 2014 (c. 6), s. 139. (6), Sch. 4 para. 62. (2)(a); S.I. 2014/889, arts. 3. (m), 7. (e)
F267. Words in s. 98. (1) inserted (1.4.2014 for specified purposes, 1.9.2014 in so far as not already in force) by Children and Families Act 2014 (c. 6), s. 139. (6), Sch. 4 para. 62. (2)(b); S.I. 2014/889, arts. 3. (m), 7. (e)
F268. Words in s. 98. (1) inserted (1.4.2014 for specified purposes, 1.9.2014 in so far as not already in force) by Children and Families Act 2014 (c. 6), s. 139. (6), Sch. 4 para. 62. (2)(c); S.I. 2014/889, arts. 3. (m), 7. (e)
F269. Words in s. 98. (1) repealed (31.3.2010) by The Apprenticeships, Skills, Children and Learning Act 2009 (Consequential Amendments) (England and Wales) Order 2010 (S.I. 2010/1080), art. 1. (3)(b)(c), Sch. 1 para. 108, Sch. 2 Pt. 3 (with art. 2. (3))
F270. S. 98. (1. A) inserted (1.4.2014 for specified purposes, 1.9.2014 in so far as not already in force) by Children and Families Act 2014 (c. 6), s. 139. (6), Sch. 4 para. 62. (3); S.I. 2014/889, arts. 3. (m), 7. (e)

Commencement Information
I93. S. 98 in force at 20.12.2006 by S.I. 2006/3360, art. 2. (e)

Termination of voluntary registration in Part B of the general childcare register on expiry of prescribed period

71. Termination of voluntary registration [F1in Part B of the general childcare register] on expiry of prescribed period
Regulations may make provision requiring the Chief Inspector to remove a registered person from Part B of the general childcare register on the expiry of a prescribed period of time from the date of his registration.

Amendments (Textual)

F1. Words in s. 71 inserted (1.4.2014 for specified purposes, 1.9.2014 in so far as not already in force) by Children and Families Act 2014 (c. 6), s. 139. (6), Sch. 4 para. 39; S.I. 2014/889, arts. 3. (m), 7. (e)
Commencement Information
I1. S. 71 in force at 20.12.2006 by S.I. 2006/3360, art. 2. (e)

Power to amend Part 3: applications in respect of multiple premises

F194. Power to amend Part 3: applications in respect of multiple premises
. . . .
Amendments (Textual)
F1. S. 94 omitted (1.1.2016) by virtue of Small Business, Enterprise and Employment Act 2015 (c. 26), s. 164. (1), Sch. 2 para. 18; S.I. 2015/1329, reg. 6. (b)

Interpretation of Part 3

98. Interpretation of Part 3.
(1) In this Part—
"the Chief Inspector" means [F1. Her Majesty's Chief Inspector of Education, Children's Services and Skills];
"childcare" has the meaning given by section 18;
[F2" childminder agency " means—
  - an early years childminder agency;
  - a later years childminder agency;]
"domestic premises" means premises which are used wholly or mainly as a private dwelling;
[F3" early years childminder agency " means a person registered in the early years register as an early years childminder agency;]
"early years provision" has the meaning given by section 96. (2);
"early years provider" has the meaning given by section 96. (3);
"early years childminding" and "early years childminder" have the meanings given by section 96. (4);
[F4" later years childminder agency " means a person registered in Part A of the general childcare register as a later years childminder agency;]
"later years provision" has the meaning given by section 96. (6);
"later years provider" has the meaning given by section 96. (7);
"later years childminding" and "later years childminder" have the meanings given by section 96. (8);
"premises" includes any area and any vehicle;
F5...
"proprietor", in relation to a school, has the same meaning as in the Education Act 1996 (c. 56);
F5...
"the Tribunal" has the meaning given by section 69. (11);
"young child" has the meaning given by section 19.
[F6. (1. A)A person is registered for the purposes of this Part if that person is registered—
  (a) in the early years register,
  (b) in the general childcare register, or
  (c) with an early years childminder agency or a later years childminder agency.]
(2) For the purposes of section 7 of the Interpretation Act 1978 (c. 30) (references to service by post), a notice or order which may by virtue of any provision of this Part be sent by post to an

applicant for registration or to a registered person is to be treated as properly addressed if it is addressed to him at the address notified by him to the Chief Inspector as the address to which correspondence to him should be sent.
Amendments (Textual)
F1. Words in s. 98. (1) substituted (1.4.2007) by Education and Inspections Act 2006 (c. 40), s. 188. (3), Sch. 14 para. 117; S.I. 2007/935, art. 5. (gg)
F2. Words in s. 98. (1) inserted (1.4.2014 for specified purposes, 1.9.2014 in so far as not already in force) by Children and Families Act 2014 (c. 6), s. 139. (6), Sch. 4 para. 62. (2)(a); S.I. 2014/889, arts. 3. (m), 7. (e)
F3. Words in s. 98. (1) inserted (1.4.2014 for specified purposes, 1.9.2014 in so far as not already in force) by Children and Families Act 2014 (c. 6), s. 139. (6), Sch. 4 para. 62. (2)(b); S.I. 2014/889, arts. 3. (m), 7. (e)
F4. Words in s. 98. (1) inserted (1.4.2014 for specified purposes, 1.9.2014 in so far as not already in force) by Children and Families Act 2014 (c. 6), s. 139. (6), Sch. 4 para. 62. (2)(c); S.I. 2014/889, arts. 3. (m), 7. (e)
F5. Words in s. 98. (1) repealed (31.3.2010) by The Apprenticeships, Skills, Children and Learning Act 2009 (Consequential Amendments) (England and Wales) Order 2010 (S.I. 2010/1080), art. 1. (3)(b)(c), Sch. 1 para. 108, Sch. 2 Pt. 3 (with art. 2. (3))
F6. S. 98. (1. A) inserted (1.4.2014 for specified purposes, 1.9.2014 in so far as not already in force) by Children and Families Act 2014 (c. 6), s. 139. (6), Sch. 4 para. 62. (3); S.I. 2014/889, arts. 3. (m), 7. (e)
Commencement Information
I1. S. 98 in force at 20.12.2006 by S.I. 2006/3360, art. 2. (e)

Part 3A Inspection of children's centres

[F1. Part 3. AInspection of children's centres

Amendments (Textual)
F1 Pt. 3. A inserted (12.1.2010) by Apprenticeships, Skills, Children and Learning Act 2009 (c. 22), ss. 199, 269. (2)

98. AInspections

(1) The Chief Inspector must—
　(a) inspect a children's centre at such intervals as may be prescribed;
　(b) inspect a children's centre at any time when the Secretary of State requires the Chief Inspector to secure its inspection.
(2) The Chief Inspector may inspect a children's centre at any other time when the Chief Inspector considers that it would be appropriate for it to be inspected.
(3) Regulations may provide that in prescribed circumstances the Chief Inspector is not required to inspect a children's centre at an interval prescribed for the purposes of subsection (1)(a).
(4) A requirement made by the Secretary of State as mentioned in subsection (1)(b) may be imposed in relation to—
　(a) children's centres generally;
　(b) a class of children's centres;
　(c) a particular children's centre.
(5) For the purposes of subsection (4)(b) a class of children's centres may be described, in particular, by reference to a geographical area.
(6) If the Chief Inspector so elects in the case of an inspection falling within subsection (1)(b) or

(2), that inspection is to be treated as if it were an inspection falling within subsection (1)(a).

98. BReports

(1) After conducting an inspection of a children's centre under section 98. A, the Chief Inspector must make a report in writing.
(2) The report must address the centre's contribution to—
    (a) facilitating access to early childhood services by parents, prospective parents and young children;
    (b) maximising the benefit of those services to parents, prospective parents and young children;
    (c) improving the well-being of young children.
(3) Regulations may make provision, for the purposes of subsection (2), about—
    (a) matters required to be dealt with in the report;
    (b) matters not required to be dealt with in the report.
(4) The regulations may, in particular, require the matters dealt with in the report to include matters relating to the quality of the leadership and management of the centre, including whether the financial resources made available to it are managed effectively.
(5) The Chief Inspector—
    (a) may send a copy of the report to the Secretary of State and must do so without delay if the Secretary of State requests a copy;
    (b) must ensure that a copy of the report is sent without delay to the relevant local authority;
    (c) may arrange for the report (or parts of it) to be further published in any manner the Chief Inspector considers appropriate.
(6) For the purposes of this section and section 98. C, the "relevant local authority", in relation to a children's centre, is the English local authority that made the arrangements under section 3. (2) by virtue of which the centre is provided.

98. CAction to be taken by local authority on receiving report

(1) This section applies where a copy of a report relating to a children's centre is sent to the relevant local authority under section 98. B(5)(b).
(2) The authority may—
    (a) send a copy of the report (or parts of it) to any person they think appropriate;
    (b) otherwise publish the report (or parts of it) in any manner they think appropriate.
(3) The authority must secure that a written statement within subsection (4) is prepared and published.
(4) A statement within this subsection is one setting out—
    (a) the action that each relevant person proposes to take in the light of the report, and
    (b) the period within which each relevant person proposes to take that action.
(5) For the purposes of this section and section 98. D, each of the following is a relevant person in relation to a children's centre—
    (a) the relevant local authority;
    (b) any person or body, other than the relevant local authority, managing the centre.
(6) In exercising their functions under this section, an English local authority must have regard to any guidance given from time to time by the Secretary of State.

98. DInspections of children's centres: powers of entry

(1) The Chief Inspector may, at any reasonable time, enter any relevant premises in England for the purpose of conducting an inspection of a children's centre under section 98. A.
(2) "Relevant premises", for the purposes of subsection (1), are—

(a) premises on which services or activities are being provided through the children's centre;
(b) premises of a relevant person which are used in connection with the staffing, organisation or operation of the children's centre.
(3) But premises used wholly or mainly as a private dwelling are not relevant premises for the purposes of subsection (1).
(4) An authorisation given by the Chief Inspector under paragraph 9. (1) of Schedule 12 to the Education and Inspections Act 2006 in relation to functions under subsection (1)—
(a) may be given for a particular occasion or period;
(b) may be given subject to conditions.
(5) Subject to any conditions imposed under subsection (4)(b), subsections (6) to (8) apply where a person ("the inspector") enters premises under this section.
(6) The inspector may—
(a) inspect the premises;
(b) take measurements and photographs or make recordings;
(c) inspect any children for whom activities are provided on the premises, and the arrangements made for their welfare;
(d) interview in private any person working on the premises who consents to be interviewed.
(7) The inspector may inspect, and take copies of, any records or documents relating to—
(a) the services or activities provided through the children's centre;
(b) the staffing, organisation or operation of the children's centre.
(8) The inspector may require a person to afford such facilities and assistance, with respect to matters within the person's control, as are necessary to enable the inspector to exercise the powers conferred by this section.
(9) Section 58 of the Education Act 2005 (inspection of computer records) applies for the purposes of this section as it applies for the purposes of Part 1 of that Act.
(10) In this section "documents" and "records" each include information recorded in any form.

98. EObstruction of power of entry, etc.

(1) A person commits an offence if the person intentionally obstructs another person exercising a power under section 98. D.
(2) A person guilty of an offence under subsection (1) is liable on summary conviction to a fine not exceeding level 4 on the standard scale.

98. FPower of constable to assist in exercise of power of entry

(1) The Chief Inspector may apply to a court for a warrant under this section.
(2) Subsection (3) applies if on an application under subsection (1) it appears to the court that the Chief Inspector—
(a) has attempted to exercise a power conferred by section 98. D but has been prevented from doing so, or
(b) is likely to be prevented from exercising any such power.
(3) The court may issue a warrant authorising any constable to assist the Chief Inspector in the exercise of the power, using reasonable force if necessary.
(4) A warrant under this section must be addressed to, and executed by, a constable.
F2. (5)..............................
[F3. (6) In this section " court " means the High Court or the family court.]
Amendments (Textual)
F2 S. 98. F(5) omitted (22.4.2014) by virtue of Crime and Courts Act 2013 (c. 22) , s. 61. (3) , Sch. 11 para. 205. (a) ; S.I. 2014/954 , art. 2. (e) (with art. 3) (with transitional provisions and savings in S.I. 2014/956 , arts. 3-11)
F3 S. 98. F(6) substituted (22.4.2014) by Crime and Courts Act 2013 (c. 22) , s. 61. (3) , Sch. 11

para. 205. (b) ; S.I. 2014/954 , art. 2. (e) (with art. 3) (with transitional provisions and savings in S.I. 2014/956 , arts. 3-11)

98. GInspection of children's centres: interpretation

In sections 98. A to 98. F—
"the Chief Inspector" means Her Majesty's Chief Inspector of Education, Children's Services and Skills;
"children's centre" has the meaning given by section 5. A(4);
"relevant partner" has the same meaning as in section 4.]

Part 4. Miscellaneous and General

Part 4. Miscellaneous and General

99. Provision of information about young children: England

(1) Regulations may make provision, in relation to England, requiring—
    (a) a person registered as an early years provider under Chapter 2 of Part 3,
    [F1. (aa)a person registered as an early years childminder agency under Chapter 2. A of Part 3,] F2...
    (b) a person who provides early years provision in respect of which, but for section 34. (2) (exemption for provision for children aged [F32] or over at certain schools), he would be required to be registered under that Chapter,[F4, and
    (c) any other person who provides early years provision for the purposes of section 1. (1) of the Childcare Act 2016 (Secretary of State's duty to secure 30 hours free childcare available for working parents),]
to provide to the relevant person such individual child information as may be prescribed.
(2) In subsection (1), "the relevant person" means one or more of the following—
    (a) the Secretary of State, and
    (b) any prescribed person.
(3) Where any person within paragraph (b) of subsection (2) receives information by virtue of subsection (1), the Secretary of State may require that person to provide any such information—
    (a) to the Secretary of State, or
    (b) to any prescribed person.
(4) The Secretary of State may provide any individual child information—
    (a) to any information collator,
    (b) to any prescribed person, or
    (c) to any person falling within a prescribed category.
(5) Any information collator—
    (a) may provide any individual child information—
(i) to the Secretary of State, or
(ii) to any other information collator, and
    (b) may at such times as the Secretary of State may determine or in prescribed circumstances provide such individual child information as may be prescribed—
(i) to any prescribed person, or
(ii) to any person falling within a prescribed category.
(6) Any person holding any individual child information (other than the Secretary of State or an information collator) may provide that information to—

(a) the Secretary of State,
(b) any information collator, or
(c) any prescribed person.

(7) No information received under or by virtue of this section shall be published in any form which includes the name of the child or children to whom it relates.

(8) Regulations under this section may provide that, in such circumstances as may be prescribed, the provision of information to a person other than the Secretary of State is to be treated, for the purposes of any provision of such regulations or this section, as compliance with any requirement imposed by or by virtue of any such provision and relating to the provision of information to the Secretary of State.

(9) In this section—

"early years provision" has the meaning given by section 20;

"individual child information" means information relating to and identifying individual children for whom early years provision is being or has been provided by a person mentioned in subsection (1)(a) or (b), whether obtained under subsection (1) or otherwise;

"information collator" means any body which, for the purposes of or in connection with the functions of the Secretary of State relating to early years provision, is responsible for collating or checking information relating to children for whom such provision is made;

F5...
F5...

Amendments (Textual)

F1. S. 99. (1)(aa) inserted (1.4.2014 for specified purposes, 1.9.2014 in so far as not already in force) by Children and Families Act 2014 (c. 6), s. 139. (6), Sch. 4 para. 63; S.I. 2014/889, arts. 3. (m), 7. (e)

F2. Word in s. 99. (1)(aa) omitted (3.11.2016) by virtue of Childcare Act 2016 (c. 5), ss. 3. (1), 7. (2); S.I. 2016/1055, reg. 2. (c)

F3. Figure in s. 99. (1)(b) substituted (26.5.2015) by Small Business, Enterprise and Employment Act 2015 (c. 26), ss. 75. (4), 164. (3)(e)

F4. S. 99. (1)(c) and word inserted (3.11.2016) by Childcare Act 2016 (c. 5), ss. 3. (1), 7. (2); S.I. 2016/1055, reg. 2. (c)

F5. Words in s. 99. (9) repealed (31.3.2010) by The Apprenticeships, Skills, Children and Learning Act 2009 (Consequential Amendments) (England and Wales) Order 2010 (S.I. 2010/1080), art. 1. (3)(b)(c), Sch. 1 para. 109, Sch. 2 Pt. 3 (with art. 2. (3))

Commencement Information

I1. S. 99 in force at 20.12.2006 for specified purposes by S.I. 2006/3360, art. 2. (d)

I2. S. 99 in force at 30.3.2007 in so far as not already in force by S.I. 2007/1019, art. 2

F6100. Provision of information about young children: transitory provision

....

Amendments (Textual)

F6. S. 100 repealed (1.9.2012) by Education Act 2011 (c. 21), ss. 1. (4), 82. (3); S.I. 2012/1087, art. 3

Commencement Information

I3. S. 100 in force at 20.12.2006 by S.I. 2006/3360, art. 2. (e)

101. Provision of information about children: Wales

(1) Regulations may make provision, in relation to Wales, requiring—
(a) a person who is registered under [F7. Part 10. A of the Children Act 1989 (c. 41)][F7. Part 2

of the Children and Families (Wales) Measure 2010] to provide child minding or day care, and
    (b) a person who provides funded nursery education,
to provide to the relevant person such individual child information as may be prescribed.
(2) In subsection (1), "the relevant person" means one or more of the following—
    (a) the Assembly, and
    (b) any prescribed person.
(3) Where any person within paragraph (b) of subsection (2) receives information by virtue of subsection (1), the Assembly may require that person to provide any such information—
    (a) to the Assembly, or
    (b) to any prescribed person.
(4) The Assembly may provide any individual child information—
    (a) to any information collator,
    (b) to any prescribed person, or
    (c) to any person falling within a prescribed category.
(5) Any information collator—
    (a) may provide any individual child information—
(i) to the Assembly, or
(ii) to any other information collator, and
    (b) may at such times as the Assembly may determine or in prescribed circumstances provide such individual child information as may be prescribed—
(i) to any prescribed person, or
(ii) to any person falling within a prescribed category.
(6) Any person holding any individual child information (other than the Assembly or an information collator) may provide that information to—
    (a) the Assembly,
    (b) any information collator, or
    (c) any prescribed person.
(7) No information received under or by virtue of this section shall be published in any form which includes the name of the child or children to whom it relates.
(8) Regulations under this section may provide that, in such circumstances as may be prescribed, the provision of information to a person other than the Assembly is to be treated, for the purposes of any provision of such regulations or this section, as compliance with any requirement imposed by or by virtue of any such provision and relating to the provision of information to the Assembly.
(9) In this section—
"child minding" and "day care" have the same meaning as in [F8. Part 10. A of the Children Act 1989][F8 Part 2 of the Children and Families (Wales) Measure 2010];
"funded nursery education" means nursery education, within the meaning of Part 5 of the School Standards and Framework Act 1998 (c. 31), which is provided by any person—
    - under arrangements made with that person by a [F9local authority] in Wales in pursuance of the duty imposed on the authority by section 118 of that Act (duty of [F9local authority] to secure sufficient nursery education), and
    - in consideration of financial assistance provided by the authority under those arrangements, other than such education provided by a school for its pupils;
"individual child information" means information relating to and identifying individual children for whom child minding, day care or funded nursery education is being or has been provided, whether obtained under subsection (1) or otherwise;
"information collator" means any body which, for the purposes of or in connection with the functions of the Assembly relating to child minding, day care or funded nursery education (as the case may be), is responsible for collating or checking information relating to children for whom such provision is made;
"prescribed" means prescribed by regulations;
"regulations" means regulations made by the Assembly.
Amendments (Textual)

F7. Words in s. 101. (1)(a) substituted (W.) (1.4.2011) by Children and Families (Wales) Measure 2010 (nawm 1), s. 75. (3), Sch. 1 para. 24. (a); S.I. 2010/2582, art. 2, Sch. 1 (with Schs. 2 3)
F8 Words in s. 101. (9) substituted (W.) (1.4.2011) by Children and Families (Wales) Measure 2010 (nawm 1) , s. 75. (3) , Sch. 1 para. 24. (b) ; S.I. 2010/2582 , art. 2 , Sch. 1 (with Schs. 2 3)
F9. Words in s. 101. (9) substituted (5.5.2010) by The Local Education Authorities and Children's Services Authorities (Integration of Functions) Order 2010 (S.I. 2010/1158), art. 1, Sch. 2 para. 58. (5)
Commencement Information
I4. S. 101 in force at 31.1.2008 by S.I. 2008/17, art. 2. (c)

Disqualification for registration under Children Act 1989.

102. Disqualification for registration under Children Act 1989.

(1) Paragraph 4 of Schedule 9. A to the Children Act 1989 (c. 41) (disqualification for registration) is amended as follows.
(2) In sub-paragraph (2)—
    (a) in paragraph (b) after "children" insert " or on grounds relating to his health ", and
    (b) after paragraph (g) insert—
"(ga)he has been given a caution in respect of any offence of a prescribed kind;".
(3) For sub-paragraph (6) substitute—
"(6)In this paragraph—
"caution" includes a reprimand or warning within the meaning of section 65 of the Crime and Disorder Act 1998;
"enactment" means any enactment having effect, at any time, in any part of the United Kingdom."
Commencement Information
I5. S. 102 in force at 20.12.2006 for E. by S.I. 2006/3360, art. 2. (f)
I6. S. 102 in force at 31.1.2008 for W. by S.I. 2008/17, art. 2. (d)

General

103. Minor and consequential amendments and repeals

(1) Schedule 2 (which contains minor and consequential amendments) has effect.
(2) The enactments specified in Schedule 3 are repealed to the extent specified.
Commencement Information
I7. S. 103 partly in force; s. 103. (1) in force at Royal Assent for certain purposes see s. 109. (1)
I8. S. 103. (1) in force at 1.4.2007 for specified purposes for E. by S.I. 2007/1019, art. 3
I9. S. 103. (1) in force at 6.4.2007 for specified purposes by S.I. 2007/1019, art. 4
I10. S. 103. (1) in force at 1.10.2007 for specified purposes by S.I. 2007/2717, art. 2. (e)
I11. S. 103. (1) in force at 1.10.2007 for specified purposes for E. by S.I. 2007/2717, art. 2. (f)
I12. S. 103. (1) in force at 1.4.2008 for specified purposes by S.I. 2008/17, art. 3. (a)
I13. S. 103. (1) in force at 1.9.2008 for specified purposes by S.I. 2008/2261, art. 2 (with Schs. 1, 2)
I14. S. 103. (2) in force at 1.4.2007 for specified purposes by S.I. 2007/1019, art. 3
I15. S. 103. (2) in force at 6.4.2007 for specified purposes by S.I. 2007/1019, art. 4
I16. S. 103. (2) in force at 1.10.2007 for specified purposes for E. by S.I. 2007/2717, art. 2. (f)
I17. S. 103. (2) in force at 1.9.2008 for specified purposes by S.I. 2008/2261, art. 2 (with Sch. 1)

104. Subordinate legislation: general provisions

(1) Any power of the Secretary of State or the Assembly to make an order or regulations under this Act is exercisable by statutory instrument.
(2) Any power of the Secretary of State or the Assembly to make an order or regulations under this Act includes power—
   (a) to make different provision for different cases or areas;
   (b) to make provision generally or in relation to specific cases;
   (c) to make such incidental, supplementary, saving or transitional provision as the Secretary of State or the Assembly thinks fit.

105. Subordinate legislation: parliamentary control

(1) A statutory instrument containing an order or regulations made by the Secretary of State under this Act is subject to annulment in pursuance of a resolution of either House of Parliament.
(2) Subsection (1) does not apply to—
   (a) an order under section 109. (2) (commencement), or
   (b) an order to which subsection (3) applies.
(3) A statutory instrument which contains (whether alone or with other provisions) —
   (a) an order under section 5,
   (b) an order under section 41. (4), or
   F10. (c)..............................
may not be made unless a draft of the instrument has been laid before, and approved by a resolution of, each House of Parliament.
Amendments (Textual)
F10. S. 105. (3)(c) omitted (1.1.2016) by virtue of Small Business, Enterprise and Employment Act 2015 (c. 26), s. 164. (1), Sch. 2 para. 19; S.I. 2015/1329, reg. 6. (b)

106. General interpretation etc.

In this Act—
"the Assembly" means the National Assembly for Wales;
"child" means a person under the age of 18;
"English local authority" means—
   - a county council in England;
   - a metropolitan district council;
   - a non-metropolitan district council for an area for which there is no county council;
   - a London borough council;
   - the Common Council of the City of London (in their capacity as a local authority);
   - the Council of the Isles of Scilly;
[F11"independent educational institution" has the same meaning as in Chapter 1 of Part 4 of the Education and Skills Act 2008;]
"maintained school" means a community, foundation or voluntary school, a community or foundation special school or a maintained nursery school;
"maintained nursery school" has the same meaning as in the School Standards and Framework Act 1998 (c. 31);
"parental responsibility" has the same meaning as in the Children Act 1989 (c. 41);
[F12"prescribed" (except in Part 2 and section 101) means prescribed by regulations;]
"registered pupil" has the same meaning as in the Education Act 1996 (c. 56);
[F12"regulations" (except in Part 2 and section 101) means regulations made by the Secretary of State;]

"school" has the same meaning as in the Education Act 1996;
"Welsh local authority" means a county council or county borough council in Wales;
"well-being", in relation to children, has the meaning given by section 1. (2).
Amendments (Textual)
F11. Words in s. 106 substituted (5.1.2015) by Education and Skills Act 2008 (c. 25), s. 173. (4), Sch. 1 para. 36; S.I. 2014/3364, art. 2. (z)
F12. Words in s. 106 inserted (31.3.2010) by The Apprenticeships, Skills, Children and Learning Act 2009 (Consequential Amendments) (England and Wales) Order 2010 (S.I. 2010/1080), art. 1. (3)(b), Sch. 1 para. 110 (with art. 2. (3))

107. Financial provisions

There shall be paid out of money provided by Parliament—
　(a) any expenses incurred by a Minister of the Crown or government department under or by virtue of this Act, and
　(b) any increase attributable to this Act in the sums which under any other Act are payable out of money so provided.

108. Isles of Scilly

Parts 1 and 3 and this Part, in their application to the Isles of Scilly, have effect subject to such exceptions, adaptations and modifications as the Secretary of State may by order prescribe.

109. Commencement

(1) The following provisions come into force on the day on which this Act is passed—
this section,
sections 104 to 108,
sections 110 and 111, and
paragraph 1 of Schedule 2 (and section 103. (1) so far as relating to that paragraph).
(2) The other provisions of this Act come into force in accordance with provision made by order by the appropriate authority (as determined under section 110).

110. The appropriate authority by whom commencement order is made

(1) This section has effect for determining who is the appropriate authority for the purposes of section 109. (2).
(2) In relation to Parts 1 and 3 (including Schedule 1) and sections 99 and 100, the appropriate authority is the Secretary of State.
(3) In relation to Part 2 and section 101, the appropriate authority is the Assembly.
(4) In relation to section 102, the appropriate authority is—
　(a) in relation to England, the Secretary of State, and
　(b) in relation to Wales, the Assembly.
(5) In relation to section 103. (1) and Schedule 2, the appropriate authority is—
　(a) for paragraphs 18. (5)(b) and (c), [F1320 to 22, 24], 27, 31, 32. (4) and 34 of that Schedule (and section 103. (1) so far as relating to those provisions)—
(i) in relation to England, the Secretary of State, and
(ii) in relation to Wales, the Assembly,
　(b) for paragraph 28 of that Schedule (and section 103. (1) so far as relating to that paragraph), the Assembly, and

(c) for the other provisions of that Schedule to which section 109. (2) applies (and section 103. (1) so far as relating to those provisions), the Secretary of State.
(6) In relation to section 103. (2) and Schedule 3, the appropriate authority is—
   (a) for a repeal contained in Part 1 of that Schedule, the Secretary of State, and
   (b) for a repeal contained in Part 2 of that Schedule, the appropriate authority for the purposes of section 109. (2) in relation to the provision on which the repeal is consequential.
Amendments (Textual)
F13. Words in s. 110. (5)(a) substituted (1.9.2009) by Learner Travel (Wales) Measure 2008 (nawm 2), s. 28. (2), Sch. 1 para. 5; S.I. 2009/371, art. 2. (2), Sch. Pt. 2

111. Short title and extent

(1) This Act may be cited as the Childcare Act 2006.
(2) Any amendment or repeal made by this Act has the same extent as the provision amended or repealed.
(3) Except as provided by subsection (2), this Act extends to England and Wales only.

Schedules

Schedule 1. Amendments relating to the curriculum

Section 48

Interpretation

1. In this Schedule "the 2002 Act" means the Education Act 2002 (c. 32).
Commencement Information
I1. Sch. 1 para. 1 in force at 1.9.2008 by S.I. 2008/2261, art. 2 (with Schs. 1, 2)

F1. . . . .

Amendments (Textual)
F1. Sch. 1 para. 2 and heading repealed (1.4.2010) by Apprenticeships, Skills, Children and Learning Act 2009 (c. 22), s. 269. (4), Sch. 16 Pt. 4; S.I. 2010/1151, art. 2, Sch. 1
F12. . . . .

Education Act 2002 (c. 32)

3. (1) Section 76 of the 2002 Act (interpretation of Part 6) is amended as follows.
(2) For the definition of "assessment arrangements" substitute—
""assessment arrangements", in relation to a key stage, means the arrangements for assessing pupils in respect of that stage for the purpose of ascertaining what they have achieved in relation to the attainment targets for that stage;".
(3) Omit the definitions of "early learning goals", "the foundation stage", and "pupil".
(4) In the definition of "school year", omit the words from "and has a corresponding" to the end.
Commencement Information

I2. Sch. 1 para. 3 in force at 1.9.2008 by S.I. 2008/2261, art. 2 (with Schs. 1, 2)

4. Omit section 77 of the 2002 Act (meaning of "nursery education" and related expressions).

Commencement Information

I3. Sch. 1 para. 4 in force at 1.9.2008 by S.I. 2008/2261, art. 2 (with Schs. 1, 2)

5. In section 78 of the 2002 Act (general requirements in relation to the curriculum), omit subsection (2).

Commencement Information

I4. Sch. 1 para. 5 in force at 1.9.2008 by S.I. 2008/2261, art. 2 (with Schs. 1, 2)

6. (1) Section 79 of the 2002 Act (duty to implement general requirements) is amended as follows.

(2) For subsections (1) and (2) substitute—

"(1) The Secretary of State shall exercise his functions with a view to securing that the curriculum for every maintained school or maintained nursery school satisfies the requirements of section 78.

(2) Every local education authority in England shall exercise their functions with a view to securing that the curriculum for every maintained school or maintained nursery school which they maintain satisfies the requirements of section 78."

(3) In subsection (4)(b), omit the words from "or the" to "nursery school".

(4) Omit subsection (5).

Commencement Information

I5. Sch. 1 para. 6 in force at 1.9.2008 by S.I. 2008/2261, art. 2 (with Schs. 1, 2)

7. (1) Section 80 of the 2002 Act (basic curriculum for maintained school) is amended as follows.

(2) In subsection (1)(b), for "who have attained the age of three" substitute " who have ceased to be young children for the purposes of Part 1 of the Childcare Act 2006 ".

(3) In subsection (2)(a), for "a nursery class in a primary school" substitute " pupils who are under compulsory school age ".

Commencement Information

I6. Sch. 1 para. 7 in force at 1.9.2008 by S.I. 2008/2261, art. 2 (with Schs. 1, 2)

8. Omit section 81 of the 2002 Act (the foundation stage).

Commencement Information

I7. Sch. 1 para. 8 in force at 1.9.2008 by S.I. 2008/2261, art. 2 (with Schs. 1, 2)

9. Omit section 83 of the 2002 Act (curriculum requirements for the foundation stage).

Commencement Information

I8. Sch. 1 para. 9 in force at 1.9.2008 by S.I. 2008/2261, art. 2 (with Schs. 1, 2)

10. (1) Section 87 of the 2002 Act (establishment of National Curriculum by order) is amended as follows.

(2) For subsection (1) substitute—

"(1) The Secretary of State shall so exercise the powers conferred by subsection (3) as to revise the National Curriculum for England whenever he considers it necessary or expedient to do so."

(3) Omit subsection (2).

(4) In subsection (4), omit—

(a) "(2) or",

(b) in paragraph (a), the words "the foundation stage or" and "educational programme or", and

(c) in paragraph (b), the words from "(or the timetables" to "education)".

(5) In subsection (5), omit "(2) or".

(6) Omit subsection (6).

(7) In subsection (8), omit "(2)(c) or".

(8) In subsection (10), omit—

(a) "(6) or", and

(b) in paragraph (a) the words from "or" to "provided".

F2. (9). . . . .

Amendments (Textual)

F2. Sch. 1 para. 10. (9) repealed (1.4.2010) by Apprenticeships, Skills, Children and Learning Act 2009 (c. 22), s. 269. (4), Sch. 16 Pt. 4; S.I. 2010/1151, art. 2, Sch. 1

Commencement Information

I9. Sch. 1 para. 10 in force at 1.9.2008 by S.I. 2008/2261, art. 2 (with Schs. 1, 2)
11. Omit section 89 of the 2002 Act (implementation in respect of nursery schools etc.).
Commencement Information
I10. Sch. 1 para. 11 in force at 1.9.2008 by S.I. 2008/2261, art. 2 (with Schs. 1, 2)
12. (1)Section 90 of the 2002 Act (development work and experiments) is amended as follows.
(2) In subsection (1), omit "or maintained nursery school".
(3) In subsection (3), omit "or a maintained nursery school".
Commencement Information
I11. Sch. 1 para. 12 in force at 1.9.2008 by S.I. 2008/2261, art. 2 (with Schs. 1, 2)
13. In section 93 of the 2002 Act (temporary exceptions for individual pupils), in subsections (1) and (5), omit "or maintained nursery school".
Commencement Information
I12. Sch. 1 para. 13 in force at 1.9.2008 by S.I. 2008/2261, art. 2 (with Schs. 1, 2)
14. In section 94 of the 2002 Act (information concerning directions under section 93), in subsection (4)(a), omit "or maintained nursery school".
Commencement Information
I13. Sch. 1 para. 14 in force at 1.9.2008 by S.I. 2008/2261, art. 2 (with Schs. 1, 2)
15. In section 96 of the 2002 Act (procedure for making certain orders and regulations), in subsection (1)(a)—
(a) omit "83. (3)", and
(b) for "87. (2)(a) or (b) or (3)(a) or (b)" substitute " 87. (3)(a) or (b) ".
Commencement Information
I14. Sch. 1 para. 15 in force at 1.9.2008 by S.I. 2008/2261, art. 2 (with Schs. 1, 2)
16. In section 210 of the 2002 Act (orders and regulations)—
(a) omit subsection (3)(c), and
(b) in subsection (5)(b), for "87. (2)(c) or (3)(c)" substitute " 87. (3)(c) ".
Commencement Information
I15. Sch. 1 para. 16 in force at 1.9.2008 by S.I. 2008/2261, art. 2 (with Schs. 1, 2)

Schedule 2. Minor and consequential amendments

Section 103. (1)

Local Authority Social Services Act 1970 (c. 42)

1. In Schedule 1 to the Local Authority Social Services Act 1970 (social services functions) after the entry relating to the Children Act 1975 insert—
"Adoption Act 1976 | Functions continuing to be exercisable by virtue of any transitional or saving provision made by or under the Adoption and Children Act 2002." |

Magistrates' Courts Act 1980 (c. 43)

F12. . . . .
Amendments (Textual)
F1. Sch. 2 para. 2 repealed (22.4.2014) by Crime and Courts Act 2013 (c. 22), s. 61. (3), Sch. 10 para. 99 Table; S.I. 2014/954, art. 2. (d) (with art. 3) (with transitional provisions and savings in S.I. 2014/956, arts. 3-11)

Supreme Court Act 1981 (c. 54)

3. In Schedule 1 to the Supreme Court Act 1981 (distribution of business in High Court) in paragraph 3 (which deals with business assigned to the Family Division) after paragraph (e) insert—
"(ea)proceedings under section 79 of the Childcare Act 2006;".
Commencement Information
I1. Sch. 2 para. 3 in force at 6.4.2007 by S.I. 2007/1019, art. 4

Children Act 1989 (c. 41)

F24. . . . .
Amendments (Textual)
F2. Sch. 2 para. 4 omitted (6.4.2016) by virtue of The Social Services and Well-being (Wales) Act 2014 (Consequential Amendments) Regulations 2016 (S.I. 2016/413), regs. 2. (1), 233
5[F3. In the heading of Part 10. A of the Children Act 1989 (child minding and day care for children in England and Wales), omit "England and".]
Amendments (Textual)
F3. Sch. 2 paras. 5-18 repealed (W.) (1.4.2011) by Children and Families (Wales) Measure 2010 (nawm 1), s. 75. (3), Sch. 2; S.I. 2010/2582, art. 2, Sch. 1 (with Schs. 2, 3)
Commencement Information
I2. Sch. 2 para. 5 in force at 1.9.2008 by S.I. 2008/2261, art. 2 (with Schs. 1, 2)
6[F3 In Part 10. A of the Children Act 1989 (including Schedule 9. A) for "the registration authority", "a registration authority" or "the authority", wherever occurring, substitute (in each case) " the Assembly " .]
Amendments (Textual)
F3. Sch. 2 paras. 5-18 repealed (W.) (1.4.2011) by Children and Families (Wales) Measure 2010 (nawm 1), s. 75. (3), Sch. 2; S.I. 2010/2582, art. 2, Sch. 1 (with Schs. 2, 3)
Commencement Information
I3. Sch. 2 para. 6 in force at 1.9.2008 by S.I. 2008/2261, art. 2 (with Schs. 1, 2)
7[F3 In section 79. B of the Children Act 1989 (other definitions etc.)—
(a) omit subsection (1),
(b) for subsection (2) substitute—
"(2) In this Act " the Assembly " means the National Assembly for Wales. ", and
(c) for subsection (7) substitute—
"(7) " Regulations " means regulations made by the Assembly. "]
Amendments (Textual)
F3. Sch. 2 paras. 5-18 repealed (W.) (1.4.2011) by Children and Families (Wales) Measure 2010 (nawm 1), s. 75. (3), Sch. 2; S.I. 2010/2582, art. 2, Sch. 1 (with Schs. 2, 3)
Commencement Information
I4. Sch. 2 para. 7 in force at 1.9.2008 by S.I. 2008/2261, art. 2 (with Schs. 1, 2)
8[F3 In section 79. C of the Children Act 1989 (regulations etc. governing child minders and day care providers), omit subsections (1), (4) and (5).]
Amendments (Textual)
F3. Sch. 2 paras. 5-18 repealed (W.) (1.4.2011) by Children and Families (Wales) Measure 2010 (nawm 1), s. 75. (3), Sch. 2; S.I. 2010/2582, art. 2, Sch. 1 (with Schs. 2, 3)
Commencement Information
I5. Sch. 2 para. 8 in force at 1.9.2008 by S.I. 2008/2261, art. 2 (with Schs. 1, 2)
9[F3. In section 79. D of the Children Act 1989 (requirement to register)—
(a) for subsection (1) substitute—
"(1)No person shall act as a child minder in Wales unless he is registered under this Part for child minding by the Assembly.",
(b) in subsection (4) omit the words "(whether the contravention occurs in England or Wales)", and

(c) in subsection (5), after "premises" insert " in Wales " .]
Amendments (Textual)
F3. Sch. 2 paras. 5-18 repealed (W.) (1.4.2011) by Children and Families (Wales) Measure 2010 (nawm 1), s. 75. (3), Sch. 2; S.I. 2010/2582, art. 2, Sch. 1 (with Schs. 2, 3)
Commencement Information
I6. Sch. 2 para. 9 in force at 1.9.2008 by S.I. 2008/2261, art. 2 (with Schs. 1, 2)
10[F3. In section 79. H of the Children Act 1989 (suspension of registration), omit subsection (3).]
Amendments (Textual)
F3. Sch. 2 paras. 5-18 repealed (W.) (1.4.2011) by Children and Families (Wales) Measure 2010 (nawm 1), s. 75. (3), Sch. 2; S.I. 2010/2582, art. 2, Sch. 1 (with Schs. 2, 3)
Commencement Information
I7. Sch. 2 para. 10 in force at 1.9.2008 by S.I. 2008/2261, art. 2 (with Schs. 1, 2)
11[F3 In section 79. K of the Children Act 1989 (protection of children in an emergency), in subsection (1) after "registered" insert " under this Part " .]
Amendments (Textual)
F3. Sch. 2 paras. 5-18 repealed (W.) (1.4.2011) by Children and Families (Wales) Measure 2010 (nawm 1), s. 75. (3), Sch. 2; S.I. 2010/2582, art. 2, Sch. 1 (with Schs. 2, 3)
Commencement Information
I8. Sch. 2 para. 11 in force at 1.9.2008 by S.I. 2008/2261, art. 2 (with Schs. 1, 2)
12[F3. Omit sections 79. N, 79. Q and 79. R of the Children Act 1989 (which relate only to England).]
Amendments (Textual)
F3. Sch. 2 paras. 5-18 repealed (W.) (1.4.2011) by Children and Families (Wales) Measure 2010 (nawm 1), s. 75. (3), Sch. 2; S.I. 2010/2582, art. 2, Sch. 1 (with Schs. 2, 3)
Commencement Information
I9. Sch. 2 para. 12 in force at 1.9.2008 by S.I. 2008/2261, art. 2 (with Schs. 1, 2)
13[F3. In section 79. S of the Children Act 1989 (general functions of the Assembly), in subsection (2) omit the words from "but the regulations" to the end of the subsection.]
Amendments (Textual)
F3. Sch. 2 paras. 5-18 repealed (W.) (1.4.2011) by Children and Families (Wales) Measure 2010 (nawm 1), s. 75. (3), Sch. 2; S.I. 2010/2582, art. 2, Sch. 1 (with Schs. 2, 3)
Commencement Information
I10. Sch. 2 para. 13 in force at 1.9.2008 by S.I. 2008/2261, art. 2 (with Schs. 1, 2)
14[F3 In section 79. U of the Children Act 1989 (rights of entry etc.) in subsection (1) omit "England or".]
Amendments (Textual)
F3. Sch. 2 paras. 5-18 repealed (W.) (1.4.2011) by Children and Families (Wales) Measure 2010 (nawm 1), s. 75. (3), Sch. 2; S.I. 2010/2582, art. 2, Sch. 1 (with Schs. 2, 3)
Commencement Information
I11. Sch. 2 para. 14 in force at 1.9.2008 by S.I. 2008/2261, art. 2 (with Schs. 1, 2)
15[F3 In section 79. V of the Children Act 1989 (function of local authorities), after "local authority" insert " in Wales " .]
Amendments (Textual)
F3. Sch. 2 paras. 5-18 repealed (W.) (1.4.2011) by Children and Families (Wales) Measure 2010 (nawm 1), s. 75. (3), Sch. 2; S.I. 2010/2582, art. 2, Sch. 1 (with Schs. 2, 3)
Commencement Information
I12. Sch. 2 para. 15 in force at 1.9.2008 by S.I. 2008/2261, art. 2 (with Schs. 1, 2)
16[F3 In section 79. W of the Children Act 1989 (requirement for certificate of suitability), in subsection (1) after "children" (in the first place where it occurs) insert " in Wales " .]
Amendments (Textual)
F3. Sch. 2 paras. 5-18 repealed (W.) (1.4.2011) by Children and Families (Wales) Measure 2010 (nawm 1), s. 75. (3), Sch. 2; S.I. 2010/2582, art. 2, Sch. 1 (with Schs. 2, 3)
Commencement Information

I13. Sch. 2 para. 16 in force at 1.9.2008 by S.I. 2008/2261, art. 2 (with Schs. 1, 2)

17[F3. In section 105 of the Children Act 1989 (interpretation) in subsection (5. A)(b) omit "England and".]

Amendments (Textual)

F3. Sch. 2 paras. 5-18 repealed (W.) (1.4.2011) by Children and Families (Wales) Measure 2010 (nawm 1), s. 75. (3), Sch. 2; S.I. 2010/2582, art. 2, Sch. 1 (with Schs. 2, 3)

Commencement Information

I14. Sch. 2 para. 17 in force at 1.9.2008 by S.I. 2008/2261, art. 2 (with Schs. 1, 2)

18 [F3. (1)Schedule 9. A to the Children Act 1989 (child minding and day care for young children) is amended as follows.

(2) In the heading, after "children" insert " in Wales " .

(3)In paragraph 1 (exemption of certain schools), in sub-paragraph (1)(c), omit "the Secretary of State or".

(4)In paragraph 4 (disqualification for registration)—

(a) in sub-paragraph (1), after "day care" insert " in Wales " ,

(b) in sub-paragraph (2)(f), after "Part XA" insert " , or Part 3 of the Childcare Act 2006, " ,

(c) in sub-paragraph (3), after "day care" (in each place where it occurs) insert " in Wales " ,

(d) in sub-paragraph (4), after "day care" (in each place where it occurs) insert " in Wales " , and

(e) in sub-paragraph (5), after "day care" (in each place where it occurs) insert " in Wales " .

(5) In paragraph 5 (offences relating to disqualification)—

(a)in sub-paragraph (1)(a)—

(i) after "child minder" insert " in Wales " ,

(ii) after "child minding" insert " in Wales " ,

(b) in sub-paragraph (1)(b) for "any of sub-paragraphs (3) to (5)" substitute " sub-paragraph (4) or (5) " , and

(c)for sub-paragraph (2) substitute—

"(2)A person who contravenes sub-paragraph (4) of paragraph 4 shall not be guilty of an offence under this paragraph if—

(a) he is disqualified for registration by virtue only of regulations made under sub-paragraph (3) of paragraph 4, and

(b) he proves that he did not know, and had no reasonable grounds for believing, that he was living in the same household as a person who was disqualified for registration or in a household in which such a person was employed."

(6) In paragraph 6 (certificates of registration), in sub-paragraph (5)—

(a) in paragraph (a) for "(in England or in Wales)" substitute " in Wales " , and

(b) in paragraph (b) after "any premises" insert " in Wales " .

(7)In paragraph 8 (co-operation between authorities), omit sub-paragraph (1).]

Amendments (Textual)

F3. Sch. 2 paras. 5-18 repealed (W.) (1.4.2011) by Children and Families (Wales) Measure 2010 (nawm 1), s. 75. (3), Sch. 2; S.I. 2010/2582, art. 2, Sch. 1 (with Schs. 2, 3)

Commencement Information

I15. Sch. 2 para. 18. (1)-(4) (5)(a) (7) in force at 1.9.2008 by S.I. 2008/2261, art. 2 (with Schs. 1, 2)

I16. Sch. 2 para. 18. (5)(b)(c) in force at 1.9.2008 for E. by S.I. 2008/2261, art. 2 (with Schs. 1, 2)

Water Industry Act 1991 (c. 56)

19. In Schedule 4. A to the Water Industry Act 1991 (premises that are not to be disconnected for non-payment of charges) for paragraph 12 substitute—

"12. (1)Premises in England which are used for the provision of childcare by a person who is registered (otherwise than as a childminder) under Part 3 of the Childcare Act 2006 in respect of the premises.

(2) Premises in Wales which are used for the provision of day care for children by a person who is registered under Part 10. A of the Children Act 1989 in respect of the premises."
Commencement Information
I17. Sch. 2 para. 19 in force at 6.4.2007 by S.I. 2007/1019, art. 4 (with art. 6, Sch. para. 4)

Education Act 1996 (c. 56)

20. In the heading to section 17 of the Education Act 1996, for "nursery education" substitute " nursery schools ".
Commencement Information
I18. Sch. 2 para. 20 in force at 1.9.2008 for E. by S.I. 2008/2261, art. 2 (with Sch. 1)
F421. . . . .
Amendments (Textual)
F4. Sch. 2 para. 21 omitted (1.9.2014) by virtue of Children and Families Act 2014 (c. 6), s. 139. (6), Sch. 3 para. 16. (4)(c); S.I. 2014/889, art. 7. (a) (with savings and transitional provisions in S.I. 2014/2270 (as amended (1.4.2015) by S.I. 2015/505)
22. (1)Section 329. A of the Education Act 1996 (review or assessment of educational needs at request of responsible body) is amended as follows.
(2) In subsection (11), for "relevant nursery education" substitute " relevant early years education ".
(3) In subsection (13)(c), for "nursery", in both places, substitute " early years ".
F5. (4). . . . .
Amendments (Textual)
F5. Sch. 2 para. 22. (4) omitted (1.9.2014) by virtue of Children and Families Act 2014 (c. 6), s. 139. (6), Sch. 3 para. 20. (4); S.I. 2014/889, art. 7. (a) (with savings and transitional provisions in S.I. 2014/2270 (as amended (1.4.2015) by S.I. 2015/505)
Commencement Information
I19. Sch. 2 para. 22 in force at 1.9.2008 for E. by S.I. 2008/2261, art. 2 (with Sch. 1)
23. In section 509. A of the Education Act 1996 (travel arrangements for children receiving nursery education otherwise than at school)—
(a) in the heading and in each of subsections (1), (3) and (4) for "nursery education" substitute " early years education ", and
(b) for subsection (5) substitute—
"(5)In this section "relevant early years education" means—
   (a) in relation to England, early years provision as defined by section 20 of the Childcare Act 2006 which is provided under arrangements made by a local authority in England in pursuance of the duty imposed by section 7 of that Act (whether or not the local authority provides the early years provision);
   (b) in relation to Wales, nursery education which is provided—
(i) by a local education authority in Wales, or
(ii) by any other person who is in receipt of financial assistance given by a local authority under arrangements made by them in pursuance of the duty imposed by section 118 of the School Standards and Framework Act 1998."
Commencement Information
I20. Sch. 2 para. 23 in force at 1.9.2008 for E. by S.I. 2008/2261, art. 2 (with Sch. 1)
24. In section 512 of the Education Act 1996 (LEA functions concerning provision of meals etc.)—
(a) in subsection (1)(c) for "relevant funded nursery education" substitute " relevant funded early years education ", and
(b) in subsection (6) for the definition of "relevant funded nursery education" substitute—
""relevant funded early years education", in relation to a local education authority in England, means early years provision as defined by section 20 of the Childcare Act 2006 which is provided

by a person, other than the governing body of a maintained school (within the meaning of section 20. (7) of the School Standards and Framework Act 1998) or a maintained nursery school, under arrangements made by a local authority in pursuance of the duty imposed by section 7 of the 2006 Act (duty to secure prescribed early years provision free of charge);

"relevant funded early years education", in relation to a local education authority in Wales, means education provided by a person other than the governing body of a maintained school (within the meaning of section 20. (7) of the School Standards and Framework Act 1998) or a maintained nursery school—

(a) under arrangements made with that person by the authority in pursuance of the duty imposed on the authority by section 118 of that Act (duty of LEA to secure sufficient nursery education), and

(b) in consideration of financial assistance provided by the authority under those arrangements."

Commencement Information

I21. Sch. 2 para. 24 in force at 1.9.2008 for E. by S.I. 2008/2261, art. 2 (with Sch. 1)

25. (1)Section 515 of the Education Act 1996 (provision of teaching services for day nurseries) is amended as follows.

(2) In subsection (1) after "a day nursery" insert " in England or Wales or to a registered early years provider in England ".

(3) In subsection (3)—

(a) in paragraph (b) after "the day nursery" insert " or (as the case may be) the registered early years provider ", and

(b) in paragraph (c) for the words from "including" to the end of the paragraph substitute "including—

(i) in relation to England, any charges to be imposed in connection with the arrangements, and

(ii) in relation to Wales, where the teacher's school and the day nursery are in the areas of different local education authorities, financial adjustments between those authorities."

(4) For subsection (4) substitute—

"(4)In this section—

"day nursery" means a day nursery provided under section 18 of the Children Act 1989 (provision by local authorities of day care for pre-school and other children);

"registered early years provider" means a person registered under Part 3 of the Childcare Act 2006."

Commencement Information

I22. Sch. 2 para. 25 in force at 1.9.2008 by S.I. 2008/2261, art. 2 (with Sch. 1)

26. (1)Section 535 of the Education Act 1996 (provision of teaching services for day nurseries) is amended as follows.

(2) In subsection (1) after "a day nursery" insert " in England or Wales or to a registered early years provider in England ".

(3) In subsection (3)—

(a) in paragraph (b) after "the day nursery" insert " or (as the case may be) the registered early years provider ", and

(b) in paragraph (c) for the words from "including" to the end of the paragraph substitute "including—

(i) in relation to England, any charges to be imposed in connection with the arrangements, and

(ii) in relation to Wales, where the teacher's school and the day nursery are in the areas of different local education authorities, financial adjustments between those authorities."

(4) For subsection (4) substitute—

"(4)In this section—

"day nursery" means a day nursery provided under section 18 of the Children Act 1989 (provision by local authorities of day care for pre-school and other children);

"registered early years provider" means a person registered under Part 3 of the Childcare Act 2006."

Commencement Information

I23. Sch. 2 para. 26 in force at 1.9.2008 by S.I. 2008/2261, art. 2 (with Sch. 1)

27. (1)Section 548 of the Education Act 1996 (no right to give corporal punishment) is amended as follows.

(2) In subsection (1)(c) for "specified nursery education" substitute " specified early years education ".

(3) For subsection (8) substitute—

"(8)"Specified early years education" means—

(a) in relation to England, early years provision as defined by section 20 of the Childcare Act 2006 which is provided under arrangements made by a local authority in England in pursuance of the duty imposed by section 7 of that Act (whether or not the local authority provides the early years provision);

(b) in relation to Wales, full-time or part-time education suitable for children who have not attained compulsory school age which is provided—

(i) by a local education authority in Wales, or

(ii) by any other person who is in receipt of financial assistance given by such an authority under arrangements made by them in pursuance of the duty imposed by section 118 of the School Standards and Framework Act 1998."

Commencement Information

I24. Sch. 2 para. 27 in force at 1.9.2008 for E. by S.I. 2008/2261, art. 2 (with Sch. 1)

Education Act 1997 (c. 44)

28. In section 38 of the Education Act 1997 (inspection of local education authorities), in subsection (2. A)(b), after "sections 25 and 26" insert " of the Children Act 2004 ".

Commencement Information

I25. Sch. 2 para. 28 in force at 1.4.2008 by S.I. 2008/17, art. 3. (b)

Police Act 1997 (c. 50)

29. In section 113. F of the Police Act 1997 (criminal record certificates: supplementary), in subsection (1)—

(a) before paragraph (a) insert—

"(za)for the purposes of Part 3 of the Childcare Act 2006 (regulation of provision of childcare in England) and regulations made under it, the applicant's suitability to look after or be in regular contact with children;",

(b) in paragraph (a), omit the words "England and", and

(c) in paragraph (c) omit the words "section 71 of the Children Act 1989 or".

Commencement Information

I26. Sch. 2 para. 29. (b)(c) in force at 1.9.2008 by S.I. 2008/2261, art. 2 (with Sch. 1)

I27. Sch. 2 para. 29. (a) in force at 6.4.2007 by S.I. 2007/1019, art. 4

School Standards and Framework Act 1998 (c. 31)

30. In section 118 of the School Standards and Framework Act 1998 (duty of LEA as respects availability of nursery education)—

(a) in subsection (1) after "a local education authority" insert " in Wales ", and

(b) in subsection (2)(b) for "the Secretary of State" substitute " the National Assembly for Wales ".

Commencement Information

I28. Sch. 2 para. 30 in force at 1.9.2008 by S.I. 2008/2261, art. 2 (with Sch. 1)

31. Section 118. A of the School Standards and Framework Act 1998 (duties of LEA in respect of

childcare) is omitted.

Commencement Information

I29. Sch. 2 para. 31 in force at 1.4.2007 for E. by S.I. 2007/1019, art. 3

32. (1)Section 119 of the School Standards and Framework Act 1998 (early years development and childcare partnerships) is amended as follows.

(2) In subsection (1), after "local education authority" insert " in Wales ".

(3) In subsection (2), for "the Secretary of State" substitute " the Assembly ".

(4) In subsection (5), omit paragraph (ab).

(5) In subsection (6), for "The Secretary of State" substitute " The Assembly ".

Commencement Information

I30. Sch. 2 para. 32. (1)-(3) (5) in force at 1.10.2007 by S.I. 2007/2717, art. 2. (e)

I31. Sch. 2 para. 32. (4) in force at 1.10.2007 for E. by S.I. 2007/2717, art. 2. (f)

33. (1)Section 122 of the School Standards and Framework Act 1998 (inspection of nursery education) is amended as follows.

(2) In the heading, after "nursery education" insert " in Wales ".

(3) In subsection (1), after "nursery education" insert " in Wales ".

Commencement Information

I32. Sch. 2 para. 33 in force at 1.9.2008 by S.I. 2008/2261, art. 2 (with Sch. 1)

34. In section 123 of the School Standards and Framework Act 1998 (children with special educational needs)—

(a) in subsections (1)(a), (2) and (3. A) for "relevant nursery education" substitute " relevant early years education ", and

(b) for subsection (4) substitute—

"(4)In this section "relevant early years education" means—

(a) in relation to England, early years provision as defined by section 20 of the Childcare Act 2006 which is provided under arrangements made by a local authority in England in pursuance of the duty imposed by section 7 of that Act (whether or not the local authority provides the early years provision);

(b) in relation to Wales, nursery education which is provided—

(i) by a local education authority in Wales, or

(ii) by any other person who is in receipt of financial assistance given by such an authority under arrangements made by them in pursuance of the duty imposed by section 118."

Commencement Information

I33. Sch. 2 para. 34 in force at 1.9.2008 for E. by S.I. 2008/2261, art. 2 (with Sch. 1)

35. In section 142 of the School Standards and Framework Act 1998 (general interpretation) for subsection (5) substitute—

"(5)For the purposes of this Act children are to be regarded as admitted to a school for nursery education if—

(a) in the case of a school in England, they are admitted for early years provision as defined by section 20 of the Childcare Act 2006 and are not, or are not to be, placed on admission in a reception class or any more senior class, and

(b) in the case of a school in Wales, if they are, or are to be, placed on admission in a nursery class."

Commencement Information

I34. Sch. 2 para. 35 in force at 1.9.2008 by S.I. 2008/2261, art. 2 (with Sch. 1)

36. (1)Schedule 26 to the School Standards and Framework Act 1998 (inspection of nursery education) is amended as follows.

(2) In the title of the Schedule after "nursery education" insert " in Wales ".

(3) In paragraph 1. (1)—

(a) in paragraph (za) after "school" (in each place where it occurs) insert " in Wales ";

(b) in paragraph (a) after "local education authority" insert " in Wales ";

(c) in paragraph (b) after "local education authority" insert " in Wales ".

(4) In paragraph 1. (2) after "local education authority" insert " in Wales ".

(5) In paragraph 1. (3)(b)(ii) after "local education authority" insert " in Wales ".
(6) In paragraph 2. (1)—
(a) omit paragraph (a), and
(b) for paragraph (c) substitute—
   "(c)"the Chief Inspector" (without more) means the Chief Inspector for Wales."
(7) For paragraph 2. (5) substitute—
"(5)In this Schedule, "well-being" in relation to children for whom nursery education is provided in Wales, is a reference to their well-being having regard to the matters mentioned in section 25. (2) of the Children Act 2004."
(8) In paragraph 3 for "the Secretary of State" substitute " the Assembly ".
(9) In paragraph 4—
(a) for "the Secretary of State" (in both places where it occurs) substitute " the Assembly ", and
(b) for "the Secretary of State's" substitute " the Assembly's ".
(10) In paragraph 5 for "the Secretary of State" substitute " the Assembly ".
(11) Omit the following—
(a) paragraph 6. A,
(b) in the cross-heading before paragraph 7, the words "6. A or",
(c) in paragraph 7, the words "6. A or",
(d) paragraph 13. A,
(e) paragraph 14. (1),
(f) in paragraph 16, the words "6. A or", and
(g) in paragraph 18, sub-paragraphs (1)(a) and (4)(a).
Commencement Information
I35. Sch. 2 para. 36 in force at 1.9.2008 by S.I. 2008/2261, art. 2 (with Sch. 1)

Protection of Children Act 1999 (c. 14)

37. In section 2. A of the Protection of Children Act 1999 (power of certain authorities to refer individuals for inclusion in list of persons considered unsuitable to work with children), in subsection (1)(a) for "or Part XA of the Children Act 1989" substitute " , Part 10. A of the Children Act 1989 or Part 3 of the Childcare Act 2006 ".
Commencement Information
I36. Sch. 2 para. 37 in force at 6.4.2007 by S.I. 2007/1019, art. 4
38. In section 9 of the Protection of Children Act 1999 (the Tribunal), in subsection (2)—
(a) omit the "or" at the end of paragraph (e), and
(b) at the end of paragraph (f) insert "or
   (g) on an appeal under, or by virtue of, Part 3 of the Childcare Act 2006."
Commencement Information
I37. Sch. 2 para. 38 in force at 6.4.2007 by S.I. 2007/1019, art. 4

Criminal Justice and Court Services Act 2000 (c. 43)

39. In section 36 of the Criminal Justice and Court Services Act 2000 (meaning of "regulated position") in subsection (13) for paragraph (c) substitute—
   "(c)in relation to England—
(i) a person registered under Part 3 of the Childcare Act 2006, otherwise than as a childminder, for providing care on premises on which the child is cared for,
(ii) a person registered under Part 3 of that Act as a childminder who is providing early years or later years childminding (within the meaning of that Part of that Act) for the child,
   (ca) in relation to Wales, a person registered under Part 10. A of the Children Act 1989 for providing day care on premises on which the child is cared for, and".
Commencement Information

I38. Sch. 2 para. 39 in force at 6.4.2007 by S.I. 2007/1019, art. 4 (with art. 6, Sch. para. 5)

40. In section 42 of the Criminal Justice and Court Services Act 2000 (interpretation of Part 2) in subsection (1) for the definition of "day care premises" substitute—

""day care premises" means—

(a) in relation to England, premises in respect of which a person is registered, otherwise than as a childminder, under Part 3 of the Childcare Act 2006,

(b) in relation to Wales, premises in respect of which a person is registered under Part 10. A of the Children Act 1989 for providing day care,".

Commencement Information

I39. Sch. 2 para. 40 in force at 6.4.2007 by S.I. 2007/1019, art. 4 (with art. 6, Sch. para. 6)

Education Act 2002 (c. 32)

41. In section 153 of the Education Act 2002 (powers of LEA in respect of funded nursery education)—

(a) in subsection (1), after "local education authority" insert " in Wales ", and

(b) in subsection (2)(a), omit "the Secretary of State or (as respects local education authorities in Wales)".

Commencement Information

I40. Sch. 2 para. 41 in force at 1.9.2008 by S.I. 2008/2261, art. 2 (with Sch. 1)

Prospective

F642. . . . .

Amendments (Textual)

F6. Sch. 2 para. 42 repealed (1.9.2007 for E., 31.10.2010 for W.) by Education and Inspections Act 2006 (c. 40), s. 188. (3), Sch. 18 Pt. 6; S.I. 2007/1801, art. 3. (h); S.I. 2010/2543, art. 2. (m)

Children Act 2004 (c. 31)

43. In section 12 of the Children Act 2004 (information databases) in subsection (8) for paragraph (a) substitute—

"(a) a person registered under Part 3 of the Childcare Act 2006 (regulation of provision of childcare in England);".

Commencement Information

I41. Sch. 2 para. 43 in force at 6.4.2007 by S.I. 2007/1019, art. 4 (with art. 6, Sch. para. 7)

Education Act 2005 (c. 18)

44. In section 59. (1) of the Education Act 2005 (combined reports)—

(a) in paragraph (b) after "for children" insert " in Wales ",

(b) in paragraph (c) after "nursery education" insert " in Wales ",

(c) omit the "and" at the end of paragraph (c), and

(d) at the end of paragraph (d) insert "and

(e) Chapters 2 and 3 of Part 3 of the Childcare Act 2006 (regulation of early years and later years provision in England)."

Commencement Information

I42. Sch. 2 para. 44 in force at 1.9.2008 by S.I. 2008/2261, art. 2 (with Sch. 1)

Schedule 3. Repeals

Section 103. (2)

Commencement Information

I1. Sch. 3 in force at 1.4.2007 for specified purposes and in part for E by S.I. 2007/1019, art. 3 (with art. 6, Sch. para. 1)

I2. Sch. 3 in force at 6.4.2007 for specified purposes by S.I. 2007/1019, art. 4

Part 1. The curriculum

Commencement Information

I3. Sch. 3 Pt. 1 in force at 1.9.2008 in so far as not already in force by S.I. 2008/2261, art. 2 (with Sch. 1)

Short title and chapter | Extent of repeal |

In section 23—
 - in subsection (1), paragraph (c) and the word "and" immediately preceding it; and
 - subsection (2. A).

In section 76, the definitions of "early learning goals", "the foundation stage", and "pupil" and, in the definition of "school year", the words from "and has a corresponding" to the end.

Section 77.

Section 78. (2).

In section 79—
 - in subsection (4)(b), the words from "or the" to "nursery school"; and
 - subsection (5).

Section 81.

Section 83.

In section 87—
 - subsection (2);
 - in subsection (4), the words "(2) or", in paragraph (a) the words "the foundation stage or" and "educational programme or" and in paragraph (b) the words from "(or the timetables" to "education)";
 - in subsection (5), the words "(2) or";
 - subsection (6);
 - in subsection (8), the words "(2)(c) or";
 - in subsection (10), the words "(6) or" and, in paragraph (a), the words from "or" to "provided"; and
 - in subsection (11), the words "(2)(c) or" and "(6) or".

Section 89.

In section 90, in subsection (1) the words "or maintained nursery school" and in subsection (3) the words "or a maintained nursery school".

In section 93. (1) and (5), the words "or maintained nursery school".

In section 94. (4)(a), the words "or maintained nursery school".

In section 96. (1)(a), the words "83. (3),".

Section 210. (3)(c).

In Schedule 17, paragraph 1. (4) to (6).

Part 2. Other repeals

Commencement Information

I4. Sch. 3 Pt. 2 in force at 1.10.2007 for specified purposes for E. by S.I. 2007/2717, art. 2. (f)

I5. Sch. 3 Pt. 2 in force at 1.9.2008 for E. in so far as not already in force by S.I. 2008/2261, art. 2 (with Schs. 1, 2)

Short title and chapter | Extent of repeal |

In the heading of Part 10. A, the words "England and".

Section 79. B(1).

Section 79. C(1), (4) and (5).
In section 79. D(4), the words "(whether the contravention occurs in England or Wales)".
Section 79. H(3).
Section 79. N.
Sections 79. Q and 79. R.
In section 79. S(2), the words from "but the regulations" to the end of the subsection.
In section 79. U(1), the words "England or".
In section 105. (5. A)(b) the words "England and".
In Schedule 9. A—
- in paragraph 1. (1)(c), the words "the Secretary of State or", and
- paragraph 8. (1).
In section 113. F(1)—
- in paragraph (a), the words "England and", and
- in paragraph (c), the words "section 71 of the Children Act 1989 or".
Section 118. A.
Section 119. (5)(ab).
In Schedule 26—
- paragraph 2. (1)(a);
- paragraph 6. A;
- in the cross-heading before paragraph 7, the words "6. A, or";
- in paragraph 7, the words "6. A or";
- paragraph 13. A;
- paragraph 14. (1);
- in paragraph 16, the words "6. A or";
- in paragraph 18, sub-paragraphs (1)(a) and (4)(a).
Protection of Children Act 1999 (c. 14) | In section 9(2), the word "or" at the end of paragraph (e).
|
Section 149. (1).
Section 150. (1).
In section 153. (2)(a) the words "the Secretary of State or (as respects local education authorities in Wales)".
In section 18. (2), the word "and" at the end of paragraph (d).
In section 23. (3), the word "and" at the end of paragraph (b).
In section 59. (1), the word "and" at the end of paragraph (c).
In Schedule 7, paragraphs 1, 3, 4 and 10. (6).

Open Government Licence v3.0

Contains public sector information licensed under the Open Government Licence v3.0.
The full licence if available at the following address:
http://www.nationalarchives.gov.uk/doc/open-government-licence/version/3/

Printed in Great Britain
by Amazon